**A Hawksmere
Special Report**

TECHNIQUES FOR SUCCESSFUL
PUBLIC AFFAIRS CAMPAIGNS IN BUSINESS

Trevor King

published by Thorogood Ltd

© Trevor King 1995

All rights reserved. No part of this publication may be reproduced, stored in a retrieval system or transmitted in any form or by any means, electronic, photocopying, recording or otherwise without the prior permission of the publisher.

This book is sold subject to the condition that it shall not, by way of trade or otherwise, be lent, re-sold, hired out or otherwise circulated without the publisher's prior consent in any form of binding or cover other than in which it is published and without a similar condition including this condition being imposed upon the subsequent purchaser.

No responsibility for loss occasioned to any person acting or refraining from action as a result of any material in this publication can be accepted by the author or publisher.

A CIP catalogue record for this book is available from the British Library.

ISBN 1 85418 051 7

Published by Thorogood Limited, 12-18 Grosvenor Gardens
London SW1W 0DH. Thorogood Limited is part of the Hawksmere Group of Companies.

Printed in Great Britain by Printflow Limited.

The Author

Trevor King is the Principal of King Issues Management, specialising in issues argumentation and public affairs campaign planning. He was General Manager of Public Affairs at Imperial Tobacco during most of the 1980s, representing a company and an industry very much under threat from government regulation and legislation. The twin axes of Westminster/Whitehall and Brussels/Strasbourg became familiar territory, and through experience in these areas he developed a particular interest in public affairs in business.

He moved to Brussels to join an international trade organisation, where he gained considerable hands-on experience in planning and implementing public affairs campaigns in the Far East, the European Union and the USA.

His earlier career was with advertising agencies and consumer goods companies in marketing management, and at one time was head of marketing and brand management, advertising, sponsorship and product development for John Player and Sons. He was a long-time member of the Marketing Society, the Institute of Marketing and the International Advertising Association. He is an economics graduate of University College, London.

He has written very little on public affairs, with practical matters and activities having taken up his time, but he has planned programmes and chaired conferences on public affairs, from which experience he believes that there are many people out there needing help!

As a keen sportsman and angler, he advises the Anglers' Conservation Association, the Salmon and Trout Association and the England Fly-Fishing team – all of which have many issues and threats to contend with, not least those of significant public interest – pollution, water quality and conservation.

Techniques for Successful Public Affairs Campaigns in Business

Contents

Abbreviations used in this report 1

Foreword 2

1   Public Affairs Campaigns – the Context for Action

Introduction 5
The Approach 6
Timeliness 7
The Place of Issues Management 8
Threats and Issues 10
Where do Threats and Issues come from? 11
Reminders! 15

2   Understanding and Preparing for Issues and Threats

Pre-issue Preparation 17
Intelligence Systems 18
Reminders! 25
Political Appreciation 26
Reminders! 31
Research 32
Reminders! 36
The People Involved 37

Active Campaigning Techniques

Objectives 40
Strategy Considerations 41
Main Campaign Elements 45
Direct Media Advertising 45
Media Relations 46
Alliances and Coalitions 50
Reminders! 53
Lobby Management Programmes 54
Planned PR Programmes 58
Choosing an Agency 63
Reminders! 66

A Specimen Public Affairs Campaign

Background 68
Objective 69
Strategy 70
Preparatory Activities 71
Outline Plan 74
Communications Plan 75
Conclusion 76
The Future 76
Reminders! 77

Integration, Co-operation and Co-ordination

Reminders! 82

6 Building confidence

Reminders! 86

7 Some conclusions

Reminders! 89

Appendices

I   The UK Legislative Route: Parliamentary Proceedings for Passage of a Typical Bill 92

II   Notes on the European Union Legislative Powers 95

III   Further Reading/Useful References 97

Abbreviations used in this Report

AA	Advertising Association
CBI	Confederation of British Industry
COREPER	Committee of Permanent Representatives
DG	Directorate-General
DTI	Department of Trade and Industry
EU	European Union
GE	Global Enterprises (a fictitious company)
IAA	International Advertising Association
IOCU	International Organisation of Consumer Unions
IOD	Institute of Directors
IPA	Institute of Practitioners in Advertising
IPR	Institute of Public Relations
ISBA	Incorporated Society of British Advertisers
ITV	Independent Television
MP	Member of Parliament
MEP	Member of the European Parliament
NFU	National Farmer's Union
NPA	Newspaper Proprietors Association
PR	Public Relations
NGO	Non-government organisation
VAT	Value Added Tax
WHO	World Health Organisation

Foreword

Some two years ago I suggested to the people running Hawksmere Conferences that there was a loophole in the Conference market for a series on public affairs in business. The delegate response to the conferences that arose from this suggestion has been excellent, and the depth of interest a very pleasant surprise. This response has encouraged me to write this report, aimed at business-people who wish to know a little more about public affairs, and how to go about planning a public affairs campaign.

This report will not tell you why you need to run a public affairs campaign, or why you may need some advice on how to do so - I have made the assumption that the answer to the first point is staring you in the face, and the answer to the second follows the first. If this is not the case, then I suggest you are in an unusual situation, but the day will come when you will need some guidance as to what you could do.

This report is about helping business come to terms with countering the issues that it increasingly faces, and which affect the attainment of its proper commercial objectives. Business and industry are frequently threatened by the effects of government legislation and regulatory action, and for some sectors of business the problems are of particular concern.

The report marks out footsteps in considering and working towards a successful public affairs campaign. These footsteps lead in the same direction, but particular situations may influence decisions to take detours, or to jump over some of them - in other words you have to tread them according to your own circumstances.

By definition, the scope of this short report cannot possibly cover the detail of all the activities that may be involved in preparing a public affairs campaign in every particular set of circumstances. Nevertheless, I believe all the

major elements receive at least a mention, and I have set out an overall design which leads from one set of activities to another - or so it seems to me! If you follow these, and adapt them to circumstances, then you should be able to develop a comprehensive and structured campaign. Whether it is a success or not will be influenced by other factors, such as the style of the creative elements, the amount of funding and duration, and the inevitable element of luck.

Of course, there is already a book or two about public affairs campaigns, but these seem to be about campaigning by single-issue pressure-groups in the area of good causes related to the public issues of the day, and not really entirely appropriate for business. The needs of business in planning (and resourcing) public affairs campaigns seem to me very different because of the continuing complexity of issues and threats to be addressed, corporate structures and philosophies to be dealt with, and not least because there are shareholders needs and commercial objectives to be met. This report has been written as a result of my experiences in a business career, all of which has been focussed on marketing and public affairs, emphasised by the stated needs of delegates during our conferences. It is not a report just about lobbying, or research, or advertising, or public relations, or media relations - it is about all of these aspects brought together in a disciplined manner to form the basis of constructive and timely public affairs campaigns appropriate to the needs of business.

To be frank, there appears to be no one route or critical footstep to success, and there is no secret that I can pass on to you which will guarantee your campaign winning the day. At the very least, however, if you select the appropriate steps for your business and the issues it has to counter from those detailed in this report, then you have to be in with a good chance. Good luck!

Public Affairs Campaigns – the Context for Action

INTRODUCTION

THE APPROACH

TIMELINESS

THE PLACE OF ISSUES MANAGEMENT

THREATS AND ISSUES

WHERE DO THREATS AND ISSUES COME FROM?

Introduction

Perhaps the best way of looking at this report is to think of it as a bridge over often troubled waters, as a guide as to what can be done to counter threats and issues, and not as a text-book – which it is not. If you have any experience, or have been involved, in preparing or setting up public affairs campaigns then you will know that whilst some situations can be anticipated to some degree, there are many that cannot, and these are likely to be those that cause the most trouble, affecting your business plans and commercial objectives most severely.

As in war, business situations are often chaotic, and those that can retain their heads, whilst others are losing theirs, will come out ahead of the game. My aim in this report is to provide you with some guide-lines as to help you to stay ahead of the game in the area of public affairs. In this context, business needs to recognise the need for a comprehensive, disciplined and structured approach – more and more as the threat of legislation and regulation becomes increasingly prevalent.

For some sectors of business, the problems are especially acute, and public affairs matters for them is an important part of everyday management, as are associated issue management techniques. These latter techniques have been developed to enable business to support its efforts to anticipate and address the social and legislative changes – the curbs and regulations, the issues in fact, which bulk large in today's marketing environment. It is more than ironic that whilst the increasingly global nature of today's markets opens up new opportunities, business faces more legislative and regulatory barriers than formerly, and business must learn to live, and thrive, in this changing environment.

The Approach

The approach to be considered in planning a public affairs campaign can be either re-active or pro-active, or even both. For instance, it may be possible to anticipate a threat or an issue and present a number of arguments to your target audiences before the threatening law or regulation is drafted – in this sense the campaign is pro-active – you have got your arguments in first, or perhaps your support of pending or existing legislation is made more appropriate and effective. However, it may be necessary to follow this with a series of re-active activities before the threat diminishes. Clearly, if you can get in your arguments first, then you have an advantage, but too often other business priorities get in the way of an early start, and then important ground is lost.

It is also wise to consider whether it is your business alone or your industry that is under threat. The imposition of laws and regulations generally are often a threat to an industry, or at least part of an industry, and the preferred route may be for an industry-wide campaign. This in itself poses problems, particularly if there is no history of co-operation in the industry, and the bringing together of industry representatives for the purpose of countering a perceived common threat is often fraught with its own series of problems. The existence of a trade association, however much it is normally in the background of day-to-day commercial activities, should act as a catalyst for industry co-operation especially to meet an industry threat. In such cases, the trade association's principal purpose will be to act as a public affairs organisation for its members, and it may be that this in itself represents an opportunity to grow in stature and strengthen itself by attracting new members.

On the other hand, it may be decided that there is an advantage to be gained by going it alone, and this decision is often a matter of timing. Carrying industry colleagues with you to plan and fund an industry campaign may generate a degree of procrastination, as each company representative jockeys position for some real or imaginary competitive advantage. Where timeliness is of the essence, then there may be no option to going it alone, with the attendant disadvantages of funding and resourcing your own campaign.

In such circumstances, you may have the luxury of attributing "success" to your own efforts, although in most circumstances there is little to demonstrate what particular campaign, or element of a campaign, worked. Very often, the situation becomes very complex with several different campaigns, or sets of arguments, to assess. Then it become virtually impossible to show that it was your campaign alone that achieved the desired effect. You may still wish to claim the credit though, or else others will step in to do so!

Timeliness

The question of timeliness is very important. Often, too often, public affairs campaigns are not mounted until the issue has achieved too great a momentum, when it has become almost too big to handle, when legislation is about to become overwhelming. In such situations, the response of a business or industry to measures attacking its commercial interests is often defensive, re-active in fact. A realistic appraisal would determine that the argument has been lost before the campaign starts, but it may be considered necessary to continue with it for secondary reasons – employees, customers, the trade, and interested MPs are all important target audiences and like to see that "their company" is not taking the matter lying down. In any event, your campaign may well lay the groundwork of contacts and arguments for the next issue that lowers on the horizon.

The Place of Issues Management

In suitable circumstances, your campaign will be able to get off the ground before the issue becomes too overwhelming. Timeliness of approach, of presenting arguments, and lobbying at appropriate intervention points will all help to achieve success.

Since it represents the response of a business to measures counter-productive to its commercial interests, issues management is often seen as essentially defensive in nature. But, properly managed, it can provide real opportunities for competitive advantage to put you ahead of the game.

Issues Management Steps:

Expressed simply, issues management comprises:

- the establishment of an early-warning intelligence system to provide advance information about proposed changes or additions to laws and regulations, nationally or internationally. The next step is the establishment of the necessary databases and information networks to track the issues and their development.

- an appreciation of the political systems, procedures and protocol by which laws and regulations are drafted, developed and enacted, to enable timely intervention points to be identified.

- the development of programmes which ensure a thorough understanding of the issues and their likely commercial effects.

- the modification of attitudes and opinions among target audiences via a public affairs programme. Such a programme should include consideration of research of various forms, direct advertising, PR programmes, advocacy campaigns, lobbying programmes, the use of spokespersons based on the preparation and use of briefing and argumentation materials.

- the specification and acquisition of the resources and materials needed to implement a public affairs programme (including the critical element of "people"), and the setting of a timetable to match political realities.

These steps (which are developed in later chapters) represent a manner of setting up a comprehensive issues management programme, when carried through into detailed tasks. Within such a programme we can see where a public affairs programme would fit in, and it is this aspect which is the focus of this report.

Without an overall issues management programme, however, a public affairs programme by itself is unlikely to be properly conceived, or even the need for it anticipated. It is just this type of environment which can give rise to unforced crisis management!

Many, if not most, businesses will have seen the need to have set up some form of issues management system, even if it does not conform to the steps outlined above, and in assessing what needs to be done will not need to start from scratch. Additionally, many businesses will already have had some experience in running public affairs campaigns of one sort or another, and it is quite possible that this will have left them licking their wounds, or at least feeling uncomfortable with the outcome. The main reasons for this kind of situation are likely to be a lack of commitment (either in expenditure or in the duration of a campaign, often arising from a lack of confidence), inappropriate research, inaccurate targeting, and poor argumentation.

I hope to show that many of these reasons for failures can be avoided, or at least minimised, by outlining a specific way of approaching the problem and the consequential steps involved.

A public affairs campaign is nothing more or less than a comprehensive, integrated tailor-made series of activities to counter the issues that threaten the proper commercial interests of a business. In certain circumstances, such a campaign will be developed to meet anticipated threats, whilst in others it may arise through some unexpected contingency or even crisis. It is in these latter circumstances that it is particularly important to keep your head and plan an integrated and comprehensive programme of activities.

Threats and Issues

These are not difficult to list, and in fact are normally only too obvious. For the sake of clarity though, they can be defined as social, economic, or political topics that have attracted political attention and become actual or potential subjects for legislation or regulation, directly or indirectly, and which may become a threat to the commercial objectives of a business.

Experience demonstrates that emerging issues are first talked about in a "compartmentalised" form, when different groups of people refer to a subject unaware that others are doing the same. Once a certain awareness threshold has been achieved, then the media may bring the subject into "public debate", and general public awareness evolves into "public opinion". Politicians and pressure groups (often only representing a minority) then become involved. Business will have been alerted before this stage by early-warning systems (see the section in Chapter 2 on early-warning alert systems), and taken steps to prepare for action.

At this stage, public opinion may lead the issue, rather than follow it, and politicians will be particularly alert to this "cross-over" point. The arguments, or parameters, become established, and the issue tends to be discussed in absolute rather than relative terms.

Broadly speaking, issues and threats fall into four main classes:

- product pollution incidents such as at Bhopal, Chernobyl and the Exxon Valdez oil-spill in Alaska. Deliberate product pollutions such as glass in baby-food products on supermarket shelves, and pollution of natural resources such as water, or caused by nuclear installations, are also grouped here. Such matters are generally addressed by specialised crisis management techniques, and may transgress against existing legislation and/or lead to new legislation being implemented.

- government issues of the day, such as education, jobs, law-breaking and health – and which can sometimes rub off onto a business issue, eg the effect on jobs by a factory closure caused by legislation. It is often instructive (and sometimes entertaining) to see how government goes about the business of presenting its arguments and policies, and how the media reacts.

- the "great and good" issues of the day, eg drug-taking, child abuse, the aged, and the homeless, about which there is much campaigning by single-issue pressure groups, which rarely have to answer to shareholders and respond to commercial objectives.

- business and commercial issues. Regulations to restrict or open-up trade, packaging controls, advertising restrictions, taxation (especially on the oil, tobacco and alcohol industries), product liability, intellectual properties, agricultural organisations and subsidies, local regulations, and consumerist organisations can all pose a serious issue for business.

There are obviously many other issues threatening business, but I list these as examples only.

It is this last group that this report will focus on, but of course it is worth emphasising that the principles involved are generally capable of being carried over into other areas.

Where do Threats and Issues come from?

In looking at threats and issues, it is important to remember that all businesses need to anticipate them and address them, and in this sense it is important to understand where they come from, and how they arise, in order to assess and counter them. It is not always possible to determine the emergence, or source, of an issue before a certain stage, ie when it is simply a subject for discussion among unco-ordinated groups of people in an informal manner.

In a formal sense though, the main sources of threats to business are governments, whether national, or regional, such as the European Union. These institutions originate and develop legislation and regulations common to many businesses, and indeed other types of organisations. Of course, it is possible to demonstrate that there are many government departments and agencies set up to aid and assist business to achieve commercial objectives, even if it is only to give advice on how to overcome and shortcut bureaucratic procedures (themselves created by government). It is also possible to demonstrate that much legislation and regulation is set up to protect business, often from what is defined as unfair competition.

Nevertheless, it would be difficult to argue convincingly against the view that the major source of legislation that threatens business is government. That is why the substance of many public affairs campaigns is properly focused on changing government attitudes.

Of course, governments do not always draft and agree legislation on their own initiatives. Far from it! Here are some of the main groups that seek to, directly or indirectly, influence government to introduce legislation stifling business:

- non-governmental organisations (NGOs), such as the World Health Organisation (WHO), the International Union of Consumer Organisations (IOCU), a whole range of anti-business consumerist organisations, and many other agencies may wish to influence government to introduce anti-business legislation for their own purposes. Many of these agencies have a sophisticated international network to exchange information and ideas, and are organised on a national, regional and global basis. The alcohol, tobacco, pharmaceutical, oil, chemical, agricultural/farming and advertising industries, amongst others, will have a real need to monitor NGOs.

- single-issue pressure groups are formed to bring pressure on governments to introduce legislation that may be detrimental to business, either directly or indirectly. On the face of it, the cause they espouse will appear to be laudable to many, eg the protection of an allegedly minority group, but on examination may contain anti-business elements. One real difficulty with such groups is that they are generally deaf to reason, and seek to make their case in emotive terms – and which are very difficult to counter.

- activists can come in different forms, but are often individuals with a consumerist background, who claim to represent "consumers" as a group, (by "consumerist", I mean those individuals and organisations who claim that they represent many thousands of actual consumers, but in reality may have only a few hundred, or less, members). They are often associated with a single-issue pressure group, are very mobile, and spread their experience widely. Their skills lie in propaganda and the manipulation of public opinion.

- a rather different category is that of "enabling legislation". This is legislation which is already in existence in principle, and is waiting to fall on your business or industry. The recent levying of VAT on domestic fuel (catching the gas, oil and solid fuel industries out), and increases to alcohol and tobacco taxes as a result of Budget revisions are cases in point.

In looking at these sources of threats and issues, it is important to recognise that they are often characterised by sophisticated systems of communications and organisation. In many cases, these systems may well be superior to those available in many businesses, and certainly they will be supported by individuals who are highly motivated and skilled.

Often, NGOs and activists work with other agencies to promote comprehensive and well-funded programmes, forming coalitions of common interests, which may be, directly or indirectly, anti-business. On a global, regional and national basis, an excellent communications network to co-ordinate and supply data and intelligence is often available. This enables advocates to exchange experiences, to discuss tactics and arguments, and to hold briefings on a literally world-wide basis.

With this background, many NGOs can not only plan programmes and fund them, but can provide a global interlinking to move resources, funds and activists from market to market. This cross-border transfer of public affairs technology has given many NGOs and their associates skills few industries, and fewer individual businesses, can possibly hope to gain.

The point to recognise here is that it is often NGOs which develop draft legislation and bring pressure to bear on government. By the time the draft has surfaced in government circles the damage may well have been done, and so it is very important to have good and timely information on the NGO movement as it may affect your business. As an integral part of an early-warning intelligence system, an effective monitoring programme needs to be put in place, whether industry resourced, or by one business going it alone, and it is important to appreciate the pros and cons of the different routes by which this can be handled. For instance, there could be risks in grouping your interests with those of your competitors through a trade association or professional body, and you may find that you need a resource dedicated to your own specific needs. Sometimes, a public affairs consultancy or specialised research organisation can be appropriate.

In any case, there is a need to monitor government itself, nationally and regionally, eg Westminster/Whitehall and Brussels/Strasbourg, and the same resources can often be utilised in this respect. Such a resource is a key part of the "early-warning" intelligence system which every business needs in some form or other.

REMINDERS!

- **APPROACH**

- **TIMELINESS**

- **KEY "ISSUES MANAGEMENT" ELEMENTS**
  - Early warning intelligence systems
  - Understand political systems
  - Develop understanding of issues
  - Modification of opinions and attitudes
  - Acquisition of resources

- **THREATS AND ISSUES**

- **WHERE THREATS COME FROM**
  - Governments
  - NGOs
  - Pressure groups
  - Activists
  - "Enabling" legislation

- **ROUTES**
  - Networks / coalitions
  - Cross border transfers

Understanding and Preparing for Issues and Threats

PRE-ISSUE PREPARATION

INTELLIGENCE SYSTEMS

POLITICAL APPRECIATION

RESEARCH

THE PEOPLE INVOLVED

chapter 2

Understanding and Preparing for Issues and Threats

The key element in this chapter is to emphasise the need to "DO IT NOW!" Many businesses appear not to appreciate the importance of achieving an early start in preparing to fight an issue. In one particular very large high-volume business, it used to be thought quite sufficient to arrange a meeting between the Chairman and the Chancellor of the day to set out the arguments for a nil increase in taxation at the next Budget, and any thought of a structured public affairs campaign was considered inappropriate and counter-productive. It is different now of course, and has been for many years, but the real damage in terms of public opinion and political arguments was done in those early days.

The lesson here is that tomorrow is often too late! There can be no real downside to early preparation, as at the very least all concerned in the business are better informed, management is alerted and your enemies known.

Pre-issue Preparation

In looking at what can be done in terms of preparation to counter issues and threats, it is important to bear in mind that the purpose of this is to be able to assess the commercial risk involved, to understand the effect on your business or industry, and to be able to develop a plan to deal with the situation. There is little point in collecting information and monitoring government and agencies without these in mind.

What follows is an outline of some key actions that should be taken in pre-issue preparation work.

Set-up Intelligence Systems

This section outlines a number of steps which will assist in setting up an effective intelligence system – the most important single step in preparation work. However informal this may be, it should be based on information from many different sources, quite often from markets on an international or regional basis, and cover many different issues and sets of argumentation. Properly developed, such a system will require specific in-house resources, with key people having information network skills. But at the more sophisticated stage it is unlikely that your business itself will be able to handle all the steps in the collection and assessing of information, and you will probably need to consider utilising specialist agencies and consultancies, including parliamentary advisers. The monitoring of government and NGOs as they affect your business is an important part of this process.

There is a huge amount of paper about, and with so much information to be collected, screened and analysed you must be certain that such information is both comprehensive and timely. For instance, simply scanning Hansard for details of Parliamentary debates which could affect your business will not do – it is critical to have some form of insider knowledge as to which individuals, which committees, which civil servants, which political group are key to the issue of concern, and very importantly what they are all thinking and planning. Such information is unlikely to be seen in Hansard.

Early-warning Alert System

Business sometimes has difficulty in recognising the danger signals of developing threats, and it is important that each business and industry group considers what are the "key indicators", which when activated form an early-warning alert system.

Whilst local experience and practice will show variations, an exercise in identifying the key indicators in your own business, industry or markets will pay dividends. It will help you to decide whether your business or industry is sufficiently alert to developing threats, and prompt suggestions for improvement.

Listed here are some suggested key indicators to give you a start in identifying those most appropriate for your business:

- the presence of active "consumerist" groups, such as an office of IOCU
- the starting up of an activists coalition
- the existence of "enabling" legislation
- any publication of a discussion document proposing draft legislation
- undue expressions of interest by MPs or MEPs
- an interest by a civil servant in Whitehall or in the EU Commission
- public opinions and attitudes

Grouped together these key indicators could form a formidable array of danger signals. Some, of course, represent potentially serious attacks in their own right, but each should be regarded as potentially dangerous.

As a first step, it is worth checking your markets for the existence of any of these indicators. If you are able to identify any of them, then it would be wise to review the need for any preparatory work as an essential part of any campaign planning.

Data Collection

There is no question as to the need for timely, comprehensive and accurate information in order to build up your intelligence system.

In searching for sources of information, do not neglect the obvious sources of information such as Hansard, Vachers, the Civil Service Year Report, the House Magazine, Rainbow (EU), European Report and the business press.

A major category includes notes and minutes of Committee meetings in Westminster and Brussels/Strasbourg. Remember that many such meetings are open to the public, and if you go to a few of these you will know your way around, and determine at first hand the strength and disposition of arguments. Do not allow yourself to be seduced into attending all such meetings or to go to every Parliamentary plenary session in Strasbourg – leave this to your agencies and consultants who should know all the key players and when and how best to approach them – and advise you accordingly.

Then there is the question of having your own parliamentary contacts to act as information channels and as sounding boards. At some time or another you will need good contacts in the Parliaments, and it is necessary to identify those members you can work with. Many MPs and MEPs will have a natural affinity with your business or its problems, simply because there is a constituency interest, ie you have a factory or office in a particular constituency, and all your employees there are voters. It is fair to say that there are differing views on this, but experience suggests that there are advantages in getting to know such important people early, making them aware of your business and its problems by background briefings, and to do this before any serious threat or issue develops. In other words, do not wait until a problem arises and you have to start from scratch, and generally against time, to build up a relationship.

If there are few such natural affinities between your business and parliamentarians, then you will have to search in other areas, preferably through a reliable and experienced adviser to screen possible candidates for you.

Members of Select and Back-bench Committees concerned with aspects of your business are another important source of information, and these in particular may be very helpful in specific behind-the-scenes briefings, and helping to put your arguments to Ministers, (we are really talking about lobbying here!).

Databases

Whatever your resources you will find a need to establish a number of databases appropriate to your business and its threats and issues. The amount of material to be collected and analysed will, almost certainly, turn out to be much greater than may have been first thought, so make allowance for this in setting up your system.

At the very least, there will be a need to organise material under these headings:

- tracking the various issues and threats
- argumentation of various types to address the issues. This is the raw material for your background briefings and eventually for your campaigns
- contacts for networks and coalitions, with background details of key people, funding, organisation, common interests
- contacts for friends and allies, with background details of key people, funding, organisation, common interests
- your enemies. Know them well, for they will know you and your industry well. Monitor their meetings, programmes, and their activists
- parliamentary and political procedures and protocols, also the legislative timetable

Trade Associations

Trade associations, industry bodies and professional associations can be very important in the basic gathering of information and intelligence. Many industries will have these bodies already established, others will be considering the matter. There can be fewer better ways of establishing some form of industry co-operation than the identification of a common threat, and the need to counter it.

At the very least, such a body will be able to undertake certain tasks concerned with information collection in a more dedicated and more economic manner than each business in an industry going its own way. On a more positive basis, a trade association can provide a forum for constructive discussion of plans leading to concerted action on a public affairs campaign, particularly if links with EU business partners are involved, and it is necessary to plan and think "European".

A number of different trade associations are noted later in the report. Their common base is the collection, screening and analysis of information. Some are very pro-active, whilst others are of a more regulatory nature.

Consultants

There are many organisations concerned with the monitoring and collection of information and intelligence in an on-going and dedicated manner. Some of these will also act as advisers and lobbyists, and plan and implement campaigns (this aspect is dealt with more fully in chapter 3).

Some are based in the UK, others in Brussels and other EU centres, and yet others are regional or global in their information processing. Bear in mind the need to match consultants to the type and range of information you need.

Another role is to act as intermediaries to establish communications channels and to set up networks of interest. Many consultancies will have on their staff key people with relevant hands-on experience.

Almost certainly, your business will need to use consultants in some way to help keep your business informed and forewarned. It is unlikely that in-house resources alone could handle the whole task in an economic and effective way. Additionally, you may well find that the consultancy's key people have had direct political or civil service experience, or have excellent high-level contacts which will be useful to your business.

Building Alliances

Earlier I outlined the need to make an early start in identifying possible "friends". In preparation work, now is the time to build them into a worthwhile alliance with common interests.

There are many groups to consider, for instance - farmers, growers, processors, employees, trades unions, customers/clients, distributors, wholesalers/retailers, suppliers, agencies, consultancies, national and local politicians - all those organisations both upstream and downstream of your own business area and which are involved in the welfare of your business, and which are entirely or partly dependent on its commercial well-being. There may be more of these groups than first supposed so it is wise to spend some time in identifying these and coming to a common understanding of joint problems.

A word of warning though. Only go into this activity on an "eyes open" basis, as although there may be pleasant surprises, there may be unpleasant surprises also.

Background Briefings and Position Papers

These arise from the argumentation work prepared earlier, and are designed to make your target groups more informed about your business, so that in the event of specific lobbying on particular issues they are more knowledgeable. Typical target groups for such briefings would be key media representatives and politicians.

A typical background briefing paper would outline the purpose and issue, and briefly set out the various arguments, in support of or against the issue. It should conclude with a short statement of intentions and action.

It is a useful aid to setting up a meeting and will act as an aide-memoire to leave with your contact.

Such briefings have the additional advantage that your business representatives will build valuable relationships with key contacts, and develop areas of mutual interest.

Grassroots Activity

Public opinion and the attitudes of "grassroots" groups are often vital to the success of your public affairs campaigns, and although to some extent these are what you make of them (for instance, the manner in which research questions are asked) it is important to recognise that there is much that can be done to change attitudes. The benefit of this work is that public opinion, generated by grass-roots activity, can influence politicians in your favour.

In order to plan such work, the categories below will help to start with:

- set up details of your customers/clients/consumers so that you can communicate with them quickly and effectively, possibly by direct mail, or by in-pack leaflets.

- identify who your supporters may be. Local communities and politicians, organisations which benefit from your business activities, eg sports and arts bodies which may enjoy your sponsorship will all be part of this list.

- third parties. All such potential third-parties need careful briefing and sensitive treatment, but they can often speak with greater authority as an independent voice than your own business, eg academics, on selected topics.

- set up a communications programme for these grassroots elements. This will need to be done for both internal and external audiences, to demonstrate their involvement and your arguments, and this in itself is an important part of any action plan.

REMINDERS!

- **PRE-ISSUE PREPARATION**

- **DO IT NOW!**

- **SET UP INTELLIGENCE SYSTEMS**
    - Early warning alert system
    - Published data
    - Databases
    - Trade associations
    - Consultants
    - Build alliances
    - Background briefings
    - Grassroots activities
        - Customer / client base
        - Supporters
        - Third parties
        - Communications programme

Political Appreciation
Understanding Political Systems

This section is concerned with an understanding of political systems, political targets, who to approach with what materials, and when it is best to do so. It is worth emphasising again the importance of starting early – DO IT NOW! – so that arguments and attitudes do not build up against you unnecessarily, and so that your business can begin to establish credibility and a profile with decision-makers.

This section is also concerned with demonstrating the need to understand and appreciate the who, what, where and when of the various political systems that govern business activities, increasingly on a regional and global basis. It is absolutely vital to have a very considerable knowledge of the workings of the political system in your markets so that you can use this to your advantage, and so that your involvement is not counter-productive.

This is an appropriate time to make the point regarding the relativity of Westminster and Brussels. Dealing with both centres of government will probably be appropriate for your business, as the impact of both on your commercial activities, and future plans, is increasingly self-evident. Both centres must be monitored and understood in their different styles of working, and this implies a further load on your resources. To a great extent, and for most practical purposes, what follows on political appreciation applies equally to both centres of government – and also, of course, to the civil service that supports and services these centres of government.

How much attention you give to each centre is a matter for judgement, and there is a considerable argument for giving a greater weight to the Brussels/Strasbourg axis. Much, if not most, legislation which affects business has its origin in the EU, but of course, Westminster and Whitehall remain as focus points for UK lobbying activities. Additionally, for some legislation, there is much work that can be done on certain issues, such as product taxation, in the UK.

Although the EU has become increasingly dominant in proposing legislation, Community proposals are subject to prior scrutiny by the UK Parliament. Select Committees in both Houses examine and debate the proposals, and occasionally they are debated in one or both Houses. This procedure provides further opportunities to continue with lobbying activities.

It must be said that the lobbying of individual MPs and MEPs can take a great deal of time and resources, often when time is of the essence. The judgement to be made is whether this form of lobbying is useful, or whether time and resources are better spent on civil servants and Ministers ie those who frame the policies and legislation, and those who make the executive decisions. In general, the influence of individual members of parliaments is not great, although of course certain individuals will carry much greater weight than others. The important distinction to observe is whether your contacts have the potential to influence others, either directly or indirectly.

Spend your own time, and your own resources, with those who can influence others.

In the UK, the process of political lobbying, and lobbyists themselves, have come under attack and severe scrutiny recently - some of it quite unfairly. It seems probable that some new guide-lines will be established, but bear in mind that most individual parliamentarians will wish to continue gaining information that may help them in their political careers.

Intervention Points

There are two basic types of campaigning - the public, and the private, face of political lobbying. Whether or not you decide to give your campaign a public face or to conduct it privately via political decision-makers only, and there are often compelling reasons for making such a choice, politicians will still be involved and it is essential to understand the political system - the procedures and protocol - by which legislation is proposed and enacted. In the UK, for instance, there is quite a complex procedure of Committees of both Houses, and generally debates in both Houses, with the continued involvement of "Whitehall." In the EU, the legislative procedure is rather different, with the Commission, Parliament and Council heavily involved.

Although these systems may seem complex, by definition this in itself often provides opportunities for intervention, and again it is important to understand what, where and when these may be. The identification of the possible intervention points will greatly assist you in understanding the decision flow, and will be critical in appreciating when to make your best efforts. For instance, there may be a point in the discussion of a piece of proposed EU legislation when the briefing of all elements of the parliamentary decision-making process, including the Economic and Social Committee, rapporteurs and

political party and committee secretariats, is appropriate. At other times discussion with the Commission or another single element may suffice.

You will have to consider also the best location for reaching your targets, eg MPs may be seen not only in Westminster, but also in their constituencies. MEPs can be reached in Strasbourg at plenary sessions, in Brussels (and other EU centres) for committee meetings, as well as in their constituencies. Ministers and civil servants are best seen at their offices, unless some suitable informal venue is acceptable, or perhaps the offices of a third-party. Additionally, all of these can be asked to visit your business locations if appropriate, and this may have some PR/media benefit as well. If such an on-site visit can be arranged then this is likely to make the greatest impact on politicians, as then they can see for themselves the impact on your business of the issues and threats you are targeting.

Lobby Management Preparation

With an understanding of the political systems and procedures and the most suitable intervention points, you have the knowledge and means by which to consider how to plan your lobby management programme. In this context, the earlier process of information gathering and analysis will bear fruit in the drafting of argumentation and the preparation of briefing materials.

Possibly the best way to identify useful political contacts is to do so through a third-party – perhaps a consultancy or lobbying group, so that your business does not commit itself until you are satisfied with the quality of the relationship. Parliamentary contacts are not generally established for direct lobbying work though. The best lobbyist will be your own business representatives, ideally at levels to match the level of parliamentary contact, eg the Chairman to meet a Secretary-of-State or senior Minister, or a Director to meet civil servants. The Public Relations Officer is not generally regarded as a highly-placed company official!

The point here is that only the direct representatives of a business or industry can make the arguments stick. If you feel strongly about a government policy or impending legislation then go to see the Minister responsible and tell him that you will have to close a factory or move production abroad if he goes ahead. Consultants, and parliamentary contacts, can be used to set up political meetings, and help with the preparation and distribution of briefing papers. There is much more to this matter of lobbying of course, and this is dealt with in chapter 3.

The important matters here are to define the targets for lobbying, to understand how to make the best case, ie one which those concerned will listen to and act upon, and when best to do so. To do this it is necessary to think like your targets, to get into their minds, and to consider what their own agenda may be. In this context, "they" will have good reasons for not changing the status quo, and if you can make your lobbying case without upsetting this then you have a much greater chance of carrying the day.

Particularly in an EU context, it is important to think "European". Going in to lobby in any of the EU institutions on a national basis will carry little weight, but if you can go with other EU colleagues in support then you are likely to achieve greater attention to your arguments.

The over-riding concern in the minds of all your political targets will be "will it work"? Then, if it is judged likely to work, how will it work, and what opposition is it likely to attract.

Your targets will include Ministers/MPs, EU Commissioners and their Cabinets (particularly the Chef de Cabinet), Directorates-General, MEPs, and civil servants directly, and third parties, trade bodies, the media, and grass-roots organisations indirectly. Clearly, this list is not comprehensive, and your own circumstances will help to decide which others you should include in your programme.

The key elements are to decide who to approach, what to approach them with, and when. Then you have the basis for a lobbying programme, and can fit this in with the other parts of your overall campaign (see chapter 3 on lobby management programmes).

"Politicising" the Argument

Your campaign arguments will carry more weight if you are able to give them a political dimension which is important to the politicians concerned. Almost all politicians have one matter that concerns them above all others, and that is to be elected again, or to achieve higher office. For that reason they have a deep interest in the attitudes, opinions and behaviour of voters, both nationally and in their own local constituencies. Even the Prime Minister has to be elected as an MP by local constituency voters, so it is very worthwhile to consider how voters can be influenced.

This is where attention at an earlier stage to local communities, customers, clients, retailers, and employees can prove invaluable. For instance, if you are able to show that a piece of planned government policy or legislation would adversely affect your business by putting jobs at risk, particularly if this were to arise in the constituencies of the politicians you are lobbying, then you have certainly politicised the issue and gained political attention. This is a situation where the involvement of MPs who represent constituencies in which your business employs significant numbers of voters will be important. These Members (who may be members of non-government parties) can be properly expected to show opposition to government policy in this area, and will make representations to Ministers when appropriately briefed.

Other groups who will be interested in the jobs issue will include the employer/industry bodies such as the CBI, Chambers of Commerce, trades unions, employees, retailers, wholesalers, suppliers ...... all of whom can make their own political representations, and will carry great influence in doing so.

Many other issues with the potential of political visibility, ie a threat to votes, will occur to businesses under threat. Pollution incidents, taxation increases, trade threatening policies, product pricing, threats to government revenue ... can all be expected to attract political visibility.

Realistic Political Timetable

Do not try to do too much at once, even if the need to do so seems critical. An understanding of the political timetable, and the decision flow on proposed legislation, should assist in your ability to make the decisions involved in establishing the optimum timetable for your campaign.

It is fairly straightforward to chart the expected progress of a Parliamentary Bill through its various stages, and your plans must match its timing. However, if you see a twinkle in the eye of a civil servant developing into a legislative proposal, then your timing will be different and will essentially depend on good intelligence as to its progress.

The downside of poor timing will become apparent in the counter-productive attitudes and opinions of your targets, and your whole carefully planned and funded programmes will founder, possibly never to be resuscitated.

REMINDERS!

- **POLITICAL APPRECIATION**

- **WHO, WHAT, WHEN AND WHERE?**

- **KEY ELEMENTS:**
    - Understand political systems and procedures
    - Relativity "Westminster / Brussels"
    - Identify intervention points
    - Lobby management preparation
    - Politicising the arguments
    - Establish realistic political timetable

Research

Good research is a necessary pre-requisite for a successful public affairs campaign. An unsuccessful campaign is often preceded by poor research, or in extreme cases, by none at all.

Probably it should go without saying that it is critical to understand the issues, and their implications, before proceeding down the planning track, but experience shows that this understanding is not always achieved. For instance, the government's presentation and campaign on the "poll-tax" was an example of poor research which did not appear to identify the potential pitfalls, whatever the rationale for a fairer local tax may have been.

This section aims to demonstrate the need to consider whether or not to take a number of research steps. Whether you do or not is entirely your decision, but if you do not even consider the decision and approach the matter by default then your campaign is off to an unpromising start. Do not assume that simply because there is an issue to counter that you have the necessary arguments and research background.

Of course, "research" is necessary to help establish understanding of a number of fundamental matters, ie know your enemies, and to establish databases and argumentation. However, these aspects have been outlined in chapter 2, and are not detailed again here.

Establish Target Group Attitudes

This aspect is perhaps the most important form of campaign research you can do. The main factors to consider are how best to determine the attitudes and opinions of the target groups, and whether public opinion is relevant. Both of these factors will be of immense value in the planning and development of campaigns and framing the arguments to make the most effective appeal.

- a most important use of research at the planning stage is to use it to identify topics about which you and/or your industry can pronounce freely on a factual basis, and which will be sympathetic to your viewpoint. Conversely, such research may be used to identify weakpoints and fallacies in the arguments used against you, and which can be built into your campaign.

- another useful form of research is an "economic impact study" aimed at an objective assessment of the contribution of your business or industry to:

    - the socio-economic development of a market(s), identifying contributions to employment, revenues and taxes

    - where relevant, the agro-development aspects also

    - highlight the role and contribution of both local producers and international importers to the wealth of a market

    - place into perspective any conflicts between your business interests and other "public" interests

  The findings of this type of research can be presented broadly in the categories of:

    - investment and savings/revenues

    - balance of payments/exports

    - employment/jobs

- understand the issues. The key factors to consider in understanding the issue(s) confronting your business are:

    - the effects and implications for your particular business. A good information and intelligence system are not enough, though essential to an understanding, and appropriate consultations with your colleagues is called for.

  The effects on the business will generally need to be thought through by marketing, commercial and financial functions at least. Legal advisers and accountants may be able to handle the technical negotiations, particularly where such matters as pricing, trademarks and intellectual properties are concerned, but almost certainly there will be an element of public affairs (or public relations) involved at some stage.

- effects on the whole industry are equally important, and great judgement will be needed to come to a view as to whether your own business needs are paramount, or whether the impact on the industry is likely to be such that significant resources must be given to this aspect.

- effects on your competitors. These effects may vary, depending on competitive strengths and weaknesses, and it may be possible for you to gain some form of competitive edge here, if only for a limited time. For instance, a proposal for advertising restrictions in a market may affect competitors differently, with established products standing to gain an advantage over newcomers.

- commercial and economic. This is likely to be the most important factor to consider, and considerable research may be necessary to identify and determine the likely impact of an issue. Since this research will take an appreciable time to reach conclusions, and may even involve product development and testing, this only emphasises the need to start early in monitoring and information collection.

- pre-campaign research base. This is essential to any real understanding of the attitudes of target groups, and to establish a base-line against which campaign achievements can be measured. If you do not know where you are coming from, then it is very difficult to go off in the right direction. But, this step is one often missed from campaign planning on the basis that attitudes seem only too obvious – only to turn out too late that they are not obvious at all or are not known in sufficient detail.

With a pre-campaign base-line research study you are not only able to assess progress, but through this and the post-campaign research also able to convince your management colleagues that your investment in a public affairs programme was well made.

Additionally, this type of research is needed to help in the development of argumentation and other briefing materials. It will be invaluable to the consultancies and agencies working on the campaign, and if not available to them will almost certainly be proposed by them.

- post-campaign research. This will tell you whether your campaign has achieved its communications objectives, so important for assessing the need for revisions to further campaigns – if you thought that one campaign would settle the matter then you may have a shock coming!

One difficulty to deal with is that if the objective of the campaign has been met then it is very difficult to justify further research expenditure. For instance, if we suppose that the issue was one where government taxation on your product was expected say, in the next Budget, and that there was no increase announced. In these circumstances, it might be reasonable to suppose that the campaign had worked, but further thought and enquiry leads you to suppose that the reason for the nil increase was due to circumstances outside your area of influence, eg an EU agreement to harmonise taxes. In such a case, further campaigns will be necessary in future years, and the post-campaign research will be vital to the creative input to those campaigns.

- feedback to campaign development. A campaign may be planned to have a long-life if changes of attitude or opinion are part of your objectives, and then it is important to feed into the campaign development work the results of on-going research so that any changes of direction and content can be incorporated.

- further rounds of research. Almost always there is a next round of research to give feedback and a lead to further campaign developments.

REMINDERS!

- **RESEARCH**

- **KEY ELEMENTS:**
  - Establish target groups attitudes
  - Economic impact studies
  - Understand the issues
    - Effects on the business
    - Effects on the industry
    - Effects on competitors
    - Commercial / economic
  - Pre-campaign research base
  - Post-campaign research
  - Feedback to campaign development
  - Further rounds of research

The People Involved

To round off this chapter on "Understanding and Preparation", it may be helpful to note some thoughts on the in-house human resources necessary to plan and run public affairs campaigns. As far as I can see, few, if any, relevant publications refer to this vital matter, but it is key to all the planning considered in this report.

Many businesses already have public relations executives, whether press officers or Directors of the function, and it is very likely that some of these will have had some experience of public affairs. This is not really the place to get involved in the distinction between "public affairs" and "public relations", but suffice to say that at least for the purpose of this report that public relations techniques and experience have an important part to play in most fully-fledged public affairs programmes, and that people with "PR" experience are very valuable in a public affairs function. This particular aspect forms part of the next chapter.

Looking further afield, a background in consumer goods marketing before coming to public affairs, seems to me as good as many, and better than most. If people come into public affairs from marketing, then you can be sure that they have had some experience in dealing with the media, with research techniques, dealing with agencies and consultants, be used to establishing marketing plans and setting objectives, working in teams, used to advertising and public relations techniques – although they may lack a knowledge of issues and threats, and of corporate matters, but of course this knowledge is relatively easy to pick up.

My own former colleagues and some competitors came from a political office, the media (journalists), PR executives, as lawyers, from political party secretariats, from lobby consultants, from trade associations and in two notable cases as a former R&D Director and an ex-factory manager, all showing their adaptability. Ideally, it is important that your in-house people have had experience in at least one aspect of public affairs work – and very few people have had experience of more than one or two areas – and have an interest in politics and the media. If you can build a Public Affairs department with people who have had some experience in the main elements of political lobbying, PR, marketing, and the media then you have a real chance of developing a successful function.

The individuals concerned should be people who like contacting others and trying to persuade them to their viewpoint, who are capable of opening doors, and making a lobbying case themselves.

If they are thick-skinned, but also sensitive to political nuances, and can take timely action so much the better. Very often they will find that the bullets fired at them come from both sides.

Finding these paragons may prove difficult, and most businesses find people with some, but perhaps not all of the virtues.

How many people you will need, how they should be organised, and their reporting relationships is a matter for your further consideration. Bear in mind, though, that if you employ agencies and consultants then you will need people simply to communicate with them on a regular basis – and they will necessarily spend much time with them, and with the many other political and alliance contacts your business will certainly develop, if they are doing their job. Much of the time they will not be in your offices, or they shouldn't be, and so you will need to have very good communications with them and an understanding of what they are doing. This situation can put a heavy strain on your relationship with the individuals, and you will have to consider very carefully the reporting structure and procedures if you are not to bog them down, and yourself, unnecessarily.

Active Campaigning Techniques

OBJECTIVES

STRATEGY CONSIDERATIONS

MAIN CAMPAIGN ELEMENTS

CHOOSING AN AGENCY

chapter 3

Active Campaigning Techniques

With pre-issue preparation, appropriate intelligence and research leading you to assess that the issues facing you are sufficiently serious to cause a threat to the achievement of your commercial objectives, then your business needs to make a "YES/NO" decision on a public affairs campaign.

This chapter outlines the elements in active campaigning. By definition, this is a fundamental step in making your arguments known, and will involve great judgement and persistence in carrying through your plans and ensuring they have adequate funding and time to attain their objectives.

Once again – DO IT NOW! – if your early-warning system has alerted you to danger, then do not let opinions and attitudes be given time to harden against you, as they will if left without your involvement and the exposure of your arguments. This principle applies whether your interests lie in supporting a piece of legislation or in resisting it. Ideally, of course, your arguments should be known by your target groups through background briefings ahead of this time, so that it is the "enemy" that has to recover ground.

Objectives

Generally speaking, the objectives you set will entail the blocking or changing of legislative or regulatory proposals, by modifying or changing opinions and attitudes in a legitimate manner. They may also be concerned with supporting a piece of helpful legislation, but the elements of campaigning involved will be similar.

A major factor at this stage is the matter of how public your campaign should be – should it be directed at Ministers and government institutions only, should it be directed at all possible target groups, or at a more limited series of targets? Depending on the circumstances, your business will need to come to a decision on this critical matter as it will greatly influence your objectives and the style, content, reach and funding of your campaign.

A lobbying campaign may, for instance, be considered appropriate in its own right to make the case for a relatively technical regulation concerned with say, product pricing or labelling. However, it must be remembered that even on

some apparently "technical" matters, other vociferous groups may join in, eg British fishermen disputing EU regulations and defending their interests against Spanish fishermen, or the public outcry over the export of calves for veal production, possibly with some counter-productive reactions (both situations in 1994/95).

Whatever your decision in this matter though, the core of your campaign will almost certainly be directed at government, so that the key elements of intelligence, research and lobbying will remain constant. The techniques of advertising and PR will be in support of these if the decision is made to go for a more public exposure of the arguments.

Remember that you do not have to initiate a campaign, or even to go on with one, if the circumstances turn against you. There may be a time to lay low, to hug the ground, to keep a low profile, and when you judge that this stance is appropriate then haul up the drawbridge, shelter behind the ramparts and prepare the boiling oil. "No publicity" may be your aim, for instance when a scientific study attacking your business or industry is picked up by the media, and it is judged that any involvement by your interests would only add fuel to the flames and prolong the news coverage. Sitting on your hands in such situations is very difficult to sustain, but the legal advice (and your own common-sense) to do nothing else may be compelling.

Strategy Considerations

With your objectives set out clearly, there are a number of strategy considerations to bear in mind, all of which will have an important bearing on the main campaign elements.

- identify the targets. Who and what are the groups you plan to reach, and why? How do they interact together, eg constituency voters lobbying MPs, and MPs own lobbying of Ministers.

Government institutions will be the core here, whether UK or EU, often both. For instance, in the UK, MPs, Select and Back-bench committees, political party officials, Ministers, civil servants, members of the Commons and Lords

may well be amongst those groups to be included, depending on your assessment of who makes the relevant decisions, and who influences them.

For a more public campaign, there may be many groups to consider. The earlier work in establishing allies and coalitions and organising grass-root interests will now come to fruition. Direct advertising is capable of reaching all of these groups, but it will reach many who have no interest and the expenditure needed for this will be wasted. But such advocacy will be seen by the more discrete targets also and have an influence on them as well – and it is necessary to judge whether this will bring a positive or negative influence to your campaign. For instance, if you are negotiating with Ministers and officials over a delicate and sensitive matter requiring great discretion, then a public exposure of the issue or your arguments (whether "leaked" or deliberately promoted) is not going to stand you in good stead in further negotiations. Suspicions and bad feelings are the inevitable result, whichever side is responsible for the leak and you should be very sure about the benefits to you before doing so yourself. Notwithstanding this, be very alert to leaks by officials. One government department I dealt with at one time had a history of leaks at a critical negotiating stage, and we came to believe that this behaviour was so deliberate that it was tempting to feed in misleading information, but of course this step is fraught with risk.

Very often, the initial tendency is to keep the target groups quite limited. The reasons for this are sometimes because the issue is technical, but sometimes are because funds are restricted, the business concerned does not wish a higher profile, or because there is a belief that just "a word in the right ear" will have the desired effect. Whilst all of these may be valid in certain circumstances, there will be occasions when it is necessary to widen out the target groups, even to the extent of making your arguments public.

Few businesses are willing to invest funds in a public affairs campaign similar to those that they invest in the marketing and advertising campaigns for their products or services. Yet making your arguments public needs the same careful targeting of advertising media, the same duration of campaigns (possibly more), and extensive funding if the objectives are to be met. This is especially so if the arguments against your business interests have been allowed to build up over the years, in which case you will have a considerable barrier of opinions and attitudes to overcome. The leeway may have to be made up though if your commercial objectives are to be met, and this will require a particular degree of commitment.

Of course, the use of PR techniques are a proper technique for making arguments public, but it is very possible that whilst the funds needed may not

be of the same magnitude as those needed for direct advertising, the effects are likely to be less also. PR techniques though may be particularly appropriate in helping to create a more helpful atmosphere in order to help forestall legislation or regulation (this aspect is considered more fully later in this chapter).

Consideration of all the above factors will assist in identifying your target groups, essential before moving to other campaign elements.

- pro-active communications. It is important to establish that you have positive and significant arguments to present. The basic research will have assisted you to promote your arguments early – "get your retaliation in first", so that your targets understand them before the opposition can weigh in, and before their arguments can count. This will allow your business to be positioned in a positive light.

- establish positive values at the outset. In analysing the attitudes and opinions of your target groups (see chapter 2 on research), consider what values can be identified which will give your arguments an effective perspective. For instance, "unfairness", "freedom of choice" and the public's innate common-sense can often be harnessed to frame your own more particular arguments, eg the "unfairness" of the poll-tax (as it was perceived at least).

  For instance, freedom of choice is an effective framework in which to argue the case for advertising, or for a nil rate of VAT on newspapers for instance.

- politicise the arguments to appeal to politicians, and reject those which do not. For instance, it is not very effective to pursue nationalistic arguments within the EU institutions, and you will be on much stronger ground if you can show that you have the "European" industry with you. Politicians, and those advising them, will look with more interest at your arguments if they feel that they are affected personally, or their constituency is involved, or their political party or committee or political sub-group is affected.

- frame the issues in your favour. Choose the ground you wish to fight on, so that your opponents are forced to follow suit, and to their disadvantage. This consideration might apply to choosing your markets, target groups, presentation techniques, funding and duration as well as to choosing the arguments.

- multi-media. Once you have decided to go with a fully-fledged public affairs campaign, then use all available media to do so, from direct media advocacy advertising, PR techniques, and lobbying to media relations programmes and spokespersons, events, mailings, exhibitions and displays.

  Whilst there may be occasions when a particular medium requires a specific presentation and message, the key to a multi-media approach is to be consistent, and to sustain the basic message. By all means, vary the interpretation, but once you have identified the basic proposition you wish to establish stick with it!

- then there is public opinion to be considered. The first matter is to decide whether "the public" should be brought deliberately into the campaign at all – will such opinion be useful to your arguments in helping to sway the minds of politicians? Can public opinion be used as a lever to change political attitudes?

Very often public opinion is what research concludes it to be, and the type, manner, timing and context of the research can all influence the conclusions. The lesson here is to consider such matters carefully, and to use the findings only if they are in close support of your strategy. If the research findings are not able to support your strategy, then consider whether your strategy needs to be amended. At least consider doing the research again, but in a different manner this time.

Whilst it seems true that legislation is not decided by public opinion surveys, it is possible to use these to influence parliamentarians, perhaps to support or oppose a Private Member's Bill for instance.

The other main factor in considering whether to utilise public opinion is that of reaching the "public" with your arguments. The cost and duration of doing so may be prohibitive, or at least frightening, but the existing profile of the issue may help to determine this matter, and whether the media are already interested.

Main Campaign Elements

Direct Media Advertising

In this context it is perhaps more properly called "advocacy advertising", as you will be advocating a particular case(s), rather than selling a product or service. Nevertheless, the principles of conventional direct advertising apply, and you will need to be concerned with creative styles and content, the proposition, media selection, timing and targeting, research, advertisement production, and fitting in with all the other elements of your campaign.

The important advantage that direct media advertising can give to the presentation of your campaign is that of control – control of content, style and timing – all of which are difficult if not impossible to achieve through PR techniques alone. The question to ask is, "What media presentation techniques can give me the control that I need?" If this question can be answered by reference to other media, then use them, but otherwise think seriously about the direct media option.

One practical difficulty is that of addressing your target groups closely with direct media. For instance, the appropriate choice of national newspapers, whether you choose the Times or the Sun, will probably give good coverage of your key target groups, but will invariably give coverage of socio-economic groups that are unneeded, but for which your campaign funds will have to pay.

This is the point to stress the important elements of co-ordination and complementarity. Co-ordinating the different elements of your campaign applies to the appropriate use of media, but it is the complementarity aspect that is most important. Certain promotional techniques will give wide coverage with some wastage, whilst others will give a narrow band of coverage with little wastage.

To polarise this concept, lobbying techniques will reach key politicians in a discrete manner and may cost relatively little, but would not be suitable for any extension to other wider target groups. On the other hand, newspapers (and other direct media such as TV) are able to cover huge numbers of people, but are not discrete and cost relatively large sums. It may be very much a part of your campaign strategy for your arguments to be seen, by politicians, to reach large numbers and groups of people. In such circumstances politicians may feel influenced by the opinions of their constituents and other interested groups, and your research will surely help in telling them this.

Direct advocacy advertising will generally work best integrated with, and supported by, several other campaign elements, and will rarely work well as a campaigning medium by itself. It's strengths lie in the control and the wide coverage of your arguments it can give, particularly if PR techniques and media editorials are not achieving this for you.

In my experience those professional advisers who work closely with government and with particular politicians distrust direct media advertising, often claiming it to be counter-productive to their efforts. Yet, it may be these very same politicians who are influenced by the public nature of your campaign, and the apparent strength of opinion, either directly or indirectly. You have to be the judge in the end, but be very careful not to direct your case against particular individuals. There are many instances of such campaigns being counter-productive by antagonising the very people you are trying to influence.

The important factors to bear in mind with direct media advertising are:

- focus the issue
- use research to build the arguments
- know your target audiences
- present the issue in the context of the target's self-interest
- be credible and balanced in your presentation
- use several media channels
- start early and give the campaign a head-start
- ensure the campaign has time to work

Media Relations

A good media relations programme is so important to a successful public affairs campaign that it has a specific listing here as one of the main campaign elements. In addition, some parts of it are expanded in the later "Planned PR Programmes" section.

Almost always good media editorial coverage will be an important part of your campaign, and considerable thought needs to be given as to how best to achieve this. In some cases, editorial coverage will form the only back-up to your lobbying activities, and it is critical that it is planned in such a manner as it will fit in well with this.

Of course, you cannot really be in control of editorial coverage, and whatever the professionalism of your best laid plans, there will always be some circumstance quite outside your control or influence. For instance, news of natural disasters, wars, or the personal behaviour of football stars may hit the news media quite unexpectedly, and overturn your carefully laid plans and briefings. In a way, the unexpected should be expected, and your plans must be flexible enough to allow for this - this could be the moment to use the direct media advertising you have prepared and have in reserve? But of course, if it is already part of your campaign then you may have to consider intensifying it or extending its duration - much easier to do than if you had to start from scratch.

A media relations programme will include identifying the specific media (including all the electronic media) and journalists which can give your arguments appropriate coverage, the need to establish relationships with them, to understand their agenda and problems, and to work with them on a continuing basis. You should recognise early on that editors and journalists have their own timetables, and angles of coming at an issue, and moreover may well have other influences at work, such as those of your rivals, competitors or enemies, or even their proprietors. In the end, they may well have quite different views to yourself or your agencies as to what constitutes a news story or specialist feature, and it is this factor which perhaps creates the biggest source of misunderstanding between editors and journalists on the one hand, and those who wish to exercise their influence over them.

In other words, despite all your efforts it is quite possible to find that an editorial feature does not support your arguments or perhaps does not appear at all, or worse, supports rival arguments.

Much can be done to alleviate this situation arising by making an early start in building up a relationship with key people in the media. Do not wait until you have a problem and want editorial help urgently - seek to establish the basis of a relationship with key journalists by helping them to understand the background to your business or industry, and the issues and threats it has to deal with. Make a point of meeting them on a regular basis and encourage them to come to you when they need information. The entertaining circuit is one thing, but always try to meet journalists with some information which may be helpful to them, or of use to their management.

Dealing with the media (written, radio and TV) is very time-consuming and demanding. Make sure that those who deal with the media are experienced senior people who understand the needs of the media, their need to meet deadlines, and what they believe constitutes "news".

Time may be of the essence, which may be against you, but bear in mind that simply sending a press release to busy journalists is not likely to gain either coverage or friends. After all, the whole purpose of your activity is to help the media to understand the purpose and importance of your arguments, so make time available.

A few words on the timing of your media work with the other various campaign elements. Do not neglect to consider the integration of your media relations programmes with the other elements of your overall campaign. Consider when you wish the different elements to break, and what is the optimum time for them to do so. It may be more effective for certain elements to break together, or for them to break in a sequential manner to gain the greatest impact.

For instance, media briefings on your campaign could, with advantage, be timed for a day or two prior to your direct advertising campaign breaking. Such a media briefing would include the issue, your arguments and why they should be heard, an outline of the campaign and conclusions from relevant public opinion surveys.

Some suggestions for dealing with the media:

- help your contacts as much as possible by providing accurate information, and try to remain understanding of journalists opinions – something which is not always easy!

- remember that a journalist may have information not available to you, and is likely to have developed an angle before approaching you.

- do not be flattered by being approached by a journalist, as some businessmen can be, and believe that you should agree to every request for an interview. Consider the options, and ask your own questions about the interview format, who else will be taking part, and the subjects to be discussed, before provisionally agreeing.

- be properly prepared for meetings, discussions and interviews with the media. Ensure that you are up-to-date with all your arguments, and familiar with the likely questions and angles.

- generally, do not appear to favour specific media or journalists. It is a small world, and the others will find out and may be unhelpful at a later stage, or even attempt counter-productive coverage.

- do not ask for favours, and do not pressurise contacts unduly. If a first approach does not work, then try another angle, or a third-party intermediary.

- do remember that nothing is ever completely "off the record". Whilst background briefings and many discussions may be carried out on this basis, you should not be dismayed to find that apparently "confidential" information is used, perhaps at a sensitive time.

- it is unlikely that a journalist will show you a news story before it is published, and to ask for this facility may cause a rift in your relationship.

- demonstrate forthright, honest and efficient conduct to journalists and you will earn a good reputation, which is very worthwhile in developing media relations. Even in a business or industry which is under threat or unpopular, the development of a good personal reputation will stand you in good stead at some time.

Alliances and Coalitions

In the development of your campaign, preferably in the preparation work, a number of individuals, organisations and other bodies will have been identified as possible allies. Of course, it may be that such bodies do not exist, and that you have had to build them from scratch, but whatever the situation, they generally have an important part to play in advancing your arguments.

As an example of the effectiveness of alliances and coalitions the 1994/95 campaign by the animal-rights movement to block the export of livestock to Europe has demonstrated two significant dimensions:

- the involvement of a reportedly wide range of interest groups from activists such as "Compassion in Farming", political agitators such as "Class War", genuine middle-class families (often looking uncomfortable with their front-line associates), and the media. It appears that a critical mass has been created, sufficient to keep up a momentum.

- the impact of "direct action" as a means of gaining media and political attention, compared to conventional lobbying techniques.

In this very emotional atmosphere, the farmer's lobby appears to have allowed the early rounds at least to be lost through letting the opposition get in their arguments first.

The first job you have to do in your own alliance work is to identify those bodies which have (or could have) common interests with yours. Examples of these would include employees, trade unions, industry allies and allied industries, and local communities. Ideally, it is wise to establish your position with such bodies before opinions harden, and attitudes become set.

Amongst the potential candidates for an alliance you should consider for your own purposes are the various business and trade bodies, of which the following are examples only to indicate their diversity:

General business/employers organisations:

- Confederation of British Industry (CBI)
- Institute of Directors (IOD)
- Chambers of Commerce

Trade Associations:

- Advertising Association
- Brewer's Society
- Portland Group
- Scotch Whisky Association
- Tobacco Manufacturer's Association
- Food and Drink Federation
- Food Manufacturer's Federation
- Home-Grown Cereals Authority
- The Retail Consortium
- European Vending Association
- Association of the British Pharmaceutical Industry
- National Farmer's Union (NFU)
- British Medical Association (BMA)
- Newspaper Proprietor's Association

Professional Associations:

- Royal Institute of British Architects
- Association of British Travel Agents

As a result of your earlier preparation work, your intelligence system should now trigger any warnings about alliances and coalitions being set up against your interests, eg any anti-business networks in general, and any groups set up against your specific interests.

Set clear objectives for the alliances where you can, so that they interlink with your own where possible. Their value to your campaign will largely depend on the credibility and authority of their arguments with your own target groups, and this in turn generally depends on their own degree of independence.

The value of third-party arguments can be immense, and they can approach the issue(s) from other angles to your own, and therefore carry more weight. A common practical difficulty is how to achieve any degree of control over third-parties at arms length, and still preserve their independent outlook.

You may have to accept that considerable compromise is necessary, in the interests of giving greater weight to your campaign.

In terms of control, it is often easier to accept that there will be informal and formal relationships and organisations, and that this should be recognised at an early stage. There may be quite informal arrangements and agreements with grass-roots coalitions, and formal arrangements with say, scientific and academic bodies. This distinction should not be allowed to hinder your campaign planning, rather it should be understood that this is a necessary part of working with alliances, and is important in establishing credibility and an authoritative base.

REMINDERS!

- **BUILDING ALLIANCES**

- **KEY ELEMENTS:**
    - Common interests
    - Set clear objectives
    - Third party value
    - Formal / informal
    - Scientific / academic authority

Lobby Management Programmes

Here we are dealing with the art of the possible! Lobby management programmes are designed to reach Ministers, politicians and other special interest groups, and are undertaken to try and influence legislation and regulation in one way or another – for instance by the blocking or introduction of new laws, or amendments to, or in support of existing laws. This makes it important that points of view and counter-arguments are put to legislators:

- before legislation is even considered

- while legislation is being prepared and information is being collected

- even after primary legislation has been passed, to influence later legislation

Clearly, it is impractical within the scope of this report to give concise, specific advice which would cover every contingency, and the assistance of outside political/parliamentary consultants should be considered very seriously in preparing a detailed lobby management programme.

What follows here are the general principles involved in setting up a lobby management programme. Do bear in mind that it is up to you to establish the discipline and timing of a programme as such, so that events do not happen by chance, or even not at all. It is you who will need to initiate the programme, to structure it, to feed it with material, and to integrate it with the other elements of your overall public affairs campaign.

Bear in mind that many, if not most, politicians at national and regional levels welcome information and briefings on topics in which they are interested. Invariably, they do not welcome materials on other matters, and this provides an extra discipline on lobbyists.

To get started on a programme, the priority is to make a personal contact, perhaps via a concise letter or through a third-party introduction, and maintain this form of contact throughout the relationship. In meeting with politicians, you should consider the following general guide-lines and tailor them to meet your own circumstances:

- research your meeting in order to determine how your contact likes to see material and arguments presented. Talk to officials, researchers and advisers to gain advice on presenting your material, and you may be able to get some of them on your side – remember that they will be responsible for briefing their "Minister" on you and your arguments.

- contact the officials before the meeting to check whether they would like further information, so giving them the proper opportunity to prepare and update briefing papers.

- place your arguments in a context which is relevant to your target, ie present the arguments in terms of government policy, the politician's constituency interests, or the national or regional interests of his party or committee.

  The whole issue of employment/jobs is particularly fertile ground on which to plant your arguments, as all politicians are sensitive to this issue.

- since time in a meeting will be limited, be concise, and have clear statistical evidence to back up your case – charts, graphs, slides.

- concentrate on certain sections of the proposed legislation and attempt to influence them, rather than trying to cover the whole ground at once.

- when arguing against a proposal, be ready to suggest an alternative, and avoid situations aimed at backing your contact up into a corner, or into a situation in which neither of you will give way. By all means disagree, (indeed, this will be quite common) but leave the meeting on a constructive basis, with a view to reconsider, or to talk to other politicians, or to come back from another angle.

- remember that you are unlikely to win over a politician on a first attempt. Indeed you may never do so. But you are seeking to modify opinions and attitudes, so a complete U-turn may not be necessary, or at least not at one meeting.

- leave written materials that support and expand on your arguments.

- follow up after the meeting with relevant personalised information, and arrange further meetings - almost certainly they will be necessary. A word of caution - it is very easy to be caught up in the political life and timetable, and you must maintain your own sense of time discipline in dealing with such matters.

The advantages of political lobbying are clear, but there can be a disadvantage by bringing an emerging issue into the light before its time and giving it a profile too early. A decision to act, or not, should always be a careful, deliberate one, and not arrived at by default.

In terms of meeting with political groups, as distinct to individuals, it is important to recognise that local groups can warrant a certain degree of attention, particularly if it is borne in mind that such groups are generally the base of the national political system. Although the influence of such groups is not always very significant, senior national and regional politicians are likely to be sensitive to their opinions on major issues, and this provides a further intervention point for your arguments to be made. Additionally, the employees of a business or industry are likely to be members of local political parties, and could be motivated and assisted to present your campaign arguments from their own viewpoint.

In all your political lobbying work, be alert to changes to people, to positions, to political parties and their policies, and to officials. A Cabinet reshuffle or a government shake-up and changes in ministerial portfolios may well result in the disturbance of your carefully built-up relationships, and time spent in having to redeploy your resources.

Of course, you may be able to dispense with many of the above activities if you feel there is strong enough evidence to mount a legal case against a piece of proposed legislation or government action. Be sure about this though, and take very good professional advice before you make a move, as the general tendency is for politicians and civil servants to close ranks and adopt delaying tactics if they believe that a legal challenge is in the offing.

Here are some general guide-lines which it is wise to observe in lobbying:

- ensure your business or industry is represented by top ranking high-quality people when lobbying politicians, as they can be impressed by rank and titles (like many of us).

- do not be too selective in your political targeting, as all politicians believe themselves to be very important and excluding some may be counter-productive.

- do recognise the need to maintain good contacts with politicians of all political parties. It is too common a fault to build a relationship with only the government or majority party, forgetting that the Opposition can influence government, and that one day they may be the party in government.

- do identify those politicians who are known to be interested in your business and/or industry and its issues, on both a "for" and "against" basis. Watch their voting record.

- do not over-rely on simply social/entertaining contacts. Those you cultivate on a social basis may be very charming, but may not carry any authority or credibility with their peers, or worse, may not be reliable when the crunch comes.

- do familiarise yourself with the legislative decision-making process (outlined earlier), so that you plan the intervention points at which your lobbying is likely to be most effective.

- as part of your intelligence system, monitor all relevant forthcoming legislation and establish specifically which political committees and groups will be involved.

- strengthen your position when lobbying Ministers (and EU Commissioners and officials) by involving friendly/local MPs/MEPs, possibly by including them in your team to visit a Minister and his team.

Planned PR Programmes

In business there are few things more irritating, and unprofessional, than a series of poorly organised, ill-conceived, purposeless activities that are too often said to be a "PR" programme. Whatever you plan in this important area, high standards of planning, implementation, timing, and integration with the other elements of your campaign must be pre-eminent.

Above all, it is a sense of style that marks out the very good campaigns from the others.

By definition, this particular section cannot cover all of the ground on specific PR techniques, but it will outline those activities most appropriate to a public affairs campaign.

Conventionally, the PR function carries out many activities associated with, or aimed at gaining, the media coverage important to many public affairs campaigns. These include compiling media lists, press releases, designing stationery, press packs, newsletters; producing films, slides and videos; celebrity/personality appearances; compiling mailing lists and direct mail; entertainment; news conferences, meetings and seminars, functions and events. Additionally, your in-house PR function, or agency, may, or may not be, associated with the services of lobbyists, research consultants, and monitoring resources, but normally would be able to act as competent intermediaries with these important resources at least.

Amongst the PR techniques that business should be able to call upon in planning a public affairs campaign are:

- the development of alliances and coalitions, referred to earlier in this chapter. A PR agency should be able to act as an intermediary between you and the potential ally, in order to sound out attitudes, to identify common interests, to determine the strength of feeling over the issues you are concerned with, to seek out a consensus and to sustain a communications campaign with the different elements.

- the development of third-party arguments. The ability to be associated with professional, specialist and academic opinions and studies can be a very valuable asset to you, particularly if these can appear to be unrelated to your own involvement. Often though this may not be possible, and you must seek to employ those sources with a well-known pedigree, authority and professional standing to make the most effective use of these external sources of arguments.

For instance, a research study by a well-respected University or Institute into the economic impact of your industry is likely to carry considerable weight, and to provide the basis for argumentation.

- media relations programmes, detailed earlier. These are key to any series of PR activities, and the development of media mailing lists (including all the electronic media), relations with key journalists and publications, background briefings, the preparation of by-lined features, as well as specific issue briefings will all be very important to media coverage and a successful campaign.

    An important part of these programmes can be media visits to factories, offices and other places where people can be seen at work, environmental aspects demonstrated, technological equipment and processes in action, and sales/revenue being earned. Politicians are also interested in such visits as it gives them an opportunity to be seen by their voters, and their attendance may give journalists an extra incentive to attend.

- communications programmes with selected audiences.

    Such audiences may include management, employees, associated companies in a business group, trades unions, local communities around your business locations, customers, the "trade", clients, professional and trade associations....... all of these need to be considered in terms of your overall campaign, and whether they could play a useful part in its development and implementation. Some of the more frequently used forms of communications with these audiences are newsletters, in-house magazines and newspapers, mailings, local events and meetings, public lectures and talks, and exhibitions and displays.

- the recruitment, training and development of spokespersons is an aspect to which too little thought is often given in planning a campaign. The identification and recruitment of suitable people should start at an early stage, and professional training given in terms of handling the media – something else to which too little thought is often given. Your spokespersons will be key to gaining coverage in the media, or to not gaining coverage when this is desirable – there are sometimes circumstances in dealing with sensitive matters when no coverage is good news!

Professional media training can easily be arranged, and is highly recommended unless you and your spokespersons are very confident in front of the camera or in interview situations. This media training teaches people how to behave in front of the media, and other audiences, which are not always sympathetic to your business or viewpoint. The professional presenters and interviewers who generally undertake this training will demonstrate the vital importance of rehearsing arguments and counter-attacks. Do not forget that the media thrives on controversy and conflict, and indeed encourages it.

Remember that your spokespersons, whether the Chairman or PR Officer or technical specialists, will be seen by the media as representing your business and it will be judged accordingly. Do not propose your Chairman as a spokesperson, for instance, unless you know that he is well prepared and trained, familiar with interview techniques and journalists, and would like the role – otherwise the bullets will be fired at you from both sides, your personal business future will be in some doubt, and your campaign will suffer a major set-back.

- syndicated tapes and videos. In the same way that releases and letters are distributed to the media generally, interviews and other information can be recorded and distributed to the electronic media. This can be particularly useful to launch a campaign, or to meet a particular news item affecting your business, when it is possible to achieve widespread radio and TV coverage. Be sure to take professional advice on the production and distribution of such material.

Radio tapes will usually need a regional or local interest factor, perhaps a local personality, to be involved.

A link to international and national broadcast stations can be an important way to achieve widespread coverage, and specialised advice is necessary in using specific production studios and distribution facilities.

- radio and TV phone-ins and panel discussions. Often an effective way in which your spokespersons can be deployed to respond to questions put by the general public. The approach can be initiated by you, or a third-party, but be sure you are prepared and trained, and have a succinct case.

- direct mail techniques have many applications for reaching decision-makers and opinion-leaders. They are selective and easily controlled, but can be limited by mailing lists availability and inaccuracy. Some businesses will have their own mailing lists, whilst others will buy them in from specialist direct-mail houses.

  A particularly effective way of using direct-mail is when it is necessary to make, or correct, an argument quickly. In such cases the facility to personalise the mailing shot will add considerably to its effectiveness.

- exhibitions and displays. Depending on the audiences, static or mobile exhibitions can be invaluable in attracting a special or public audience. As many cities and towns have exhibitions designed to attract tourists, so many businesses can attract audiences of many types and interests. For instance, the Ideal Home Exhibition attracts public audiences interested in home-building and furnishing, the Boat Show attracts a more specialised audience, and others may attract educational interest groups.

  If you use exhibitions, be sure that they have a clear theme, are simple, and are effectively targeted and used.

- functions, events and sponsorships. Strictly speaking, these are normally the realm of specialised agencies and consultants, but are included here in view of the indirect public affairs benefits accruing from demonstrating an image, and for entertaining opportunities. It is certainly possible to devise sponsorships that make a particular appeal to your public affairs target audiences, and which you may be able to exploit for entertaining/social purposes. Sponsorship of the arts and certain sports events, for instance, gives many worthwhile opportunities to attract and entertain key politicians and media figures, both as small groups and as individuals, during which (or as a result of which) some discreet lobbying is generally possible. Nor does attendance at such events normally compromise their professional integrity, and is often favoured on the basis that spouses can be appropriately entertained also.

- a public information centre. The availability of free, easily accessed information sheets, brochures, photos and tapes may be helpful in building up a grass-roots campaign. This facility can be of particular use to a whole industry, whose members are widely scattered, and should be given a central location. The media should be informed of its existence and encouraged to make it known.

- there is one particular tactic that should be mentioned here, and that is the use of "Petitions". These are used to inform politicians, and others, of views on a major social or environmental issue, when the issue can be made to seem clear-cut (even if it isn't!). Petitions have a place as either a part of a structured public affairs campaign, or when other means of influence fail and it is necessary to raise the profile. They are very useful when the combined views of a number of individuals or groups are considered to carry weight with the recipients.

This tactic is most suited to situations where a strong factual argument exists, such as a case against taxation, the imposition of VAT, or say the closure of a factory. Typically, they call upon an end to government activity of some kind, or for some change to new or intended legislation. What counts more than mere numbers of signatures is the spread and weight of the groups and organisations involved.

In the early 1980s an alliance of tobacco interests organised a very successful consumer petition which generated over 1.5 million signatures, and was presented with accompanying media attention to 10, Downing Street. It was part of an integrated public affairs campaign to counter further taxation increases on tobacco – the campaign worked, for a time.

All the above PR activities are properly the responsibility of your in-house function(s), and indirectly their own advisers, consultants and agencies. All the activities have specialist aspects, and your function must be staffed by experienced, professional people. Do not place inexperienced people in positions where they interact with the media and the public – you would not do this with your key customers and suppliers, it is bad business practice.

Choosing an Agency

You are going to be working with agencies and consultants of various types. Of course, it is highly likely that you will already have agencies and consultants working with several of your functions, particularly marketing, PR and legal, and these may well be very suitable to work with you in the public affairs area – but they may not, or they may need to be augmented.

In the event that this is the case then how should you go about this very important matter? Almost certainly you will not be starting from scratch, and indeed it may be through working with say, an advertising agency, that the concept of a public affairs campaign has been mooted. Names of various agencies and consultants will probably be known to you or to your trade colleagues, and others will suggest themselves as you pursue your enquiries. What is needed is to be quite sure about what you are looking for, and to be clear on the criteria you are going to judge them.

Specifically not discussed here is the selection of legal advisers. The reason is because legal skills tend to be very discrete, and in my experience generally contribute little to the creative aspects of a campaign – indeed sometimes quite the opposite. Nevertheless, the advice of legal colleagues and their associates is essential to your campaign's well-being in terms of advising on risks and clearing actions and copy. Of course, there are circumstances where the input of legal advisers is all important, such as in the drafting of materials referring to product labelling, intellectual property rights.......or when a legal challenge can be mounted, in which circumstances considerable creativity may be needed.

What follows are some thoughts and guide-lines that have arisen from having been through the selection process quite a few times.

Firstly, identify the specialist areas in which you need outside specialist advice and work. These areas are likely to be research, advertising, PR, lobbying, monitoring, parliamentary advice, media relations and legal advice. Having done this, then put a short list together from your own knowledge, look for visual evidence of campaigns you respect, talk to the professional bodies such as the Institute of Practitioners in Advertising (IPA), the Institute of Public Relations (IPR), check in the directories, read the trade press, check for competitive conflicts and start to visit one or two. At this stage, you will be getting background, refining your own briefs and starting to ask the right questions.

Whether you go to see agencies like Saatchis or Adman, Luncher, Writer & Partners be sure why you are going to see them. You will almost certainly learn a good deal from such exploratory visits but don't waste your time, and theirs, by not having an agenda to check against.

Second, make it clear to yourself, at least, what you are looking for. Think about the following factors:

- who will you be meeting? Are they the same people who will be working on your account? If not, insist that the agency puts up the people who would work with you and your team. Are they people who run the agency or have shares in it? Be prepared to spend some time on this aspect as many cases of falling out in an agency relationship can be put down to the relationship between individuals, the chemistry.

    How experienced are these people? What do they know/who do they know?
    Make sure the agency team includes all the skills you will need. In terms of political/parliamentary advisers, the team should include people who have political party or civil service experience, perhaps having worked in a Downing Street or a Minister's private office, and who have excellent current political contacts. They should certainly include people who know their way round the corridors in all the relevant political centres.

- the agency should be able to show you examples of their work in the relevant areas of interest. Discuss with them their views on your business and the issues you are facing.

- how do they respond to your brief? Does it fall within their experience? What examples can they show?

- is the agency good at information collection and analysis? What experience does it have in monitoring political and current events, and in applying them to your business? Connections with NGOs, parliamentary groups, politicians and the media will all be useful.

    If you need EU centres to be monitored, or campaigns to run in several markets, then beware of working with an agency which works only in the UK (although it may have "associates" in the EU), unless your in-house functions can handle all the co-ordination that will be necessary.

- above all – DO IT NOW! Ideally, do not wait until you have a problem to deal with – your agency(ies), and you, will benefit from an on-going relationship, so that the agency understands your business and the relevant issues before jumping in at the deep end. Whatever the experience of the agency in other areas, they will need to make their own mistakes in your business, and you will have to allow them time to do this. In direct advertising terms at least, perhaps the first six months should be seen as a trial period for judging their ability to take a brief, the quality and style of their creative development work, and how they go about assessing this in research terms.

  If you are considering changing agencies, then allow for a cross-over period, during which time your current agency carries on as normal, until such time as you judge the new agency is ready to take over. Do not start with a new agency without any current back-up support.

- for public affairs activities, ie covering a wide range of work, it is unlikely that you will find all the services you require under one roof. In the end, you will need out-house agencies/consultants in a number of specialist areas, and you will need to be prepared to find the necessary in-house resources to handle the continuous briefing, co-ordination and assessment of their work.

As to which agencies and consultants you should use, bear in mind the old axiom of horses for courses. If you are planning a big City takeover, or even a privatisation launch, then you will need a very different agency than if you are planning a low-profile political lobbying campaign or simply a series of direct-mail shots to customers. In the end, choose an agency you and your team feel comfortable with, and whose work has some relationship with your needs.

REMINDERS!

- **ACTIVE CAMPAIGNING**

- **START EARLY!**

- **OBJECTIVE: TO MODIFY OPINIONS AND ATTITUDES**

- **STRATEGY CONSIDERATIONS:**
    - Identity targets
    - Pro-active communications
    - Establish positive values
    - Politicise the arguements
    - Frame the issues
    - Multi-media
    - Public opinion

- **MAIN CAMPAIGN ELEMENTS**
    - Direct media advertising
    - Media briefings
    - Alliances / coalitions
    - Lobby management programmes
    - Planned PR programmes

A Specimen Public Affairs Campaign

BACKGROUND

OBJECTIVE

STRATEGY

PREPARATORY ACTIVITIES

OUTLINE PLAN

COMMUNICATIONS PLAN

CONCLUSION

THE FUTURE

Specimen Public Affairs Campaign

In planning this chapter, I have looked for an issue which is realistic and which would give the opportunity to illustrate many, if not all, of the steps that have been detailed in previous chapters – moreover, one in which there would be a wide interest across many businesses, products and services groups. It is not a case-history as such, as whilst these often make for informative reading and entertaining presentation, they are often difficult to relate to specific business issues with a widespread concern. Whilst what follows is fictitious, it is based on a real issue of concern, and one which ought to be of potential interest to almost every business.

Background

From deep in Fortress Europe, parliamentary advisers have signalled that there is a growing concern over the advertising of certain product groups, ie confectionery, alcohol, toys, tobacco, pharmaceuticals and financial services. Apparently, the concern is focussed on the expenditure, contents and appeal of advertising for these product groups, some aspects of which are judged to be against the interests of consumers. There is talk of restrictions or even an outright ban. This is the issue.

In our hypothetical business, Global Enterprises (GE is a multi-product group), this news has been anticipated through an early-warning system, which a few months ago had picked up that a number of MEPs had met with various consumerist organisations in Geneva and the subject of advertising had been on the agenda. At the moment, it appears that only a few MEPs, and some Commission officials (a classic danger signal!), are interested but it seems clear to GE that it will not be long before others become involved, and specifically in UK parliamentary circles as well.

This issue is of great concern to GE, as the business development plans include the launch of a number of new brands in the EU, all of which need heavy-weight advertising support as a key part of the marketing effort. GE feels that any threat to the freedom to advertise must be resisted, and by all the companies and organisations in the advertising industry as well as the other businesses and industries that are threatened.

In practice, much of the work detailed below takes place with and through the various trade associations of which GE businesses are members. In the circumstances described, other businesses in the same industry, and in the other threatened industries too, perceive the same degree of threat and their joint actions carry greater weight with the decision-makers than one business, industry, or even market, alone. GE's experience in dealing with EU issues (and EU officials), leads to a requirement to bring the relevant European business interests together to form an alliance across Europe. This will carry significantly greater weight in the EU than a single business or even a single country.

For the purpose of this specimen campaign, the name "GE" should be taken to mean GE and its associated companies, other businesses in the same industries, and the trade associations of which they are members.

Objective

- to counter any legislation to ban or severely curtail the commercial freedoms available to GE, by modifying opinions and attitudes with those who will make the legislative decisions.

At this early stage, it is quite practicable to consider activities which would be aimed at blocking any moves to prepare draft legislation, but GE believes that, in practice, the threat will materialise and so the planning goes ahead.

Strategy

- to create a wide-ranging alliance of interests, including media-owners, advertisers, and advertising agencies, all of which would lose considerable revenues and/or have their commercial objectives placed in jeopardy as a consequence of an advertising ban, and who will promote a campaign to strengthen the positive arguments for advertising, and to correct perceived opinions and attitudes against advertising.

- to persuade the advertising industry to fund and run a campaign promoting the raison d'etre of advertising. As an indirect strategy, this is designed to demonstrate that there are positive virtues to advertising.

- to target UK and EU politicians and civil servants with arguments designed to demonstrate that a ban would be an anti-business move with serious consequences. In this sense, the need to politicise the issue is important.

- to focus on the key arguments of marketing freedoms and freedom of information.

Preparatory Activities:

- identifying the legislative powers held by the EU institutions and the UK government. This will help GE to decide on the political intervention points.

- identifying the legislative routes and political procedures likely to be involved. GE's parliamentary advisers are familiar with both the UK and EU legislative process, and the possible intervention points. They set to work to plan a specific lobbying timetable.

- identifying the common interests that are held by potential members of the planned alliance. Exploratory talks are held with representatives of the media: the Newspaper Proprietors Association (NPA), individual press owners, TV network owners/contractors and Outdoor advertising organisations.

And with representatives of advertisers: CBI, Chambers of Commerce, Incorporated Society of British Advertisers (ISBA), the Advertising Association (AA), the International Advertising Association (IAA).

And with representatives of advertising agencies, the Institute of Practitioners in Advertising (IPA), and the equivalent European organisation in particular.

Through all the UK organisations, their EU equivalents are informed of the threat, and of the action planned in the UK. It is clear that the threat is already being taken very seriously in other EU countries, and a considerable amount of work has already taken place, similar to that being planned in the UK.

Additionally, everyday business relationships are used to explore attitudes with advertising agencies with whom GE works, with key suppliers, important trade customers, and with specific media owners with whom GE places substantial advertising revenues.

- identifying the common ground with the above groups. GE finds out that this common ground is not the same with the various groups, but nevertheless there is a common core of interest in defending the right to advertise.

- updating lists of personal contacts, including political contacts, Commissioners, civil servants and advisers, freedom/liberty groups, trade unions, trade organisations, academic bodies and advertising/media groups.

- updating argumentation and briefing materials. GE finds that there is a considerable store of material, including academic studies, already on the shelf, some of it specifically concerned with the effects of advertising. GE's advisers are reviewing the need for original studies to be initiated.

- select and brief the necessary outside consultants, including a research agency, an advertising agency, and a PR agency, all of whom need up-to-date knowledge of the political process and experience in advocacy campaigning. Fortunately, the current advertising and PR agencies used by GE's marketing function have this background and were thought to be appropriate. Had this not been the case valuable time would have been taken up in selecting, briefing and bedding-down new agencies. Additionally, the current parliamentary advisers are associated with a political lobbying company, and GE has concluded that it can work with this organisation also.

- the research agency is given the task of determining the attitudes and opinions held on advertising by the key decision-makers. This establishes a base-line from which the campaign is planned, and which will provide a yard-stick against which to assess the achievements of the campaign.

Research findings will also be valuable in determining any favourable opinions and attitudes, which can then be merchandised via the communications programmes.

In this context, the value of economic impact studies (outlined earlier) in determining the adverse impact of a possible advertising ban on jobs, revenue, and trade can be immense. It is decided to go ahead with such a study by an authoritative economic research agency, and the findings will be introduced through media conferences and into direct media advertising.

- in addition, GE has decided that the importance of the issue and the complexity of the campaign requires a dedicated organising team and support staff to brief, direct and co-ordinate. Executives with political, advertising and lobbying experience are seconded to the team from within GE's associated companies. They will be responsible for developing and co-ordinating both internal and external communications activities. In particular, they will act as a team of spokespersons for GE in dealing with the media.

Outline Plan

A number of activities are detailed below indicating the scope of the activities considered appropriate and the nature of the tasks involved. It is likely that, in practice, they would be refined and streamlined.

Timing is of the essence and a campaign has to run literally as soon as possible. This is a normal situation in dealing with issues, and emphasises the importance of earlier preparatory work.

- targets are defined as politicians and civil servants who will make the legislative decision, and those groups and individuals who can influence them directly or indirectly. Specifically, these are key Ministers and officials at the DTI, the Home Office, the Department of the Environment, and possibly the Department of Health in the UK......in the EU, Directorate-General X, and possibly DGs II, III, and IV. These, together with their relevant civil servants, including COREPER (the Committee of Permanent Representatives) will form the core of the political targets.

    On a more indirect level, targets include specific parliamentary committees, such as the Environment Committee in the European Parliament (where the discussion first took place, as reported by GE's parliamentary advisers). Some of the members of this Committee (and the secretariat) are already known to GE management, and plans are made to contact them.

    The media is also a target for the arguments to be exposed. By carrying supportive editorial material, the legislative decision-makers will see the arguments from another angle. Additionally, the general public will be made aware of the issue and the arguments, and will be able to influence politicians. Note - it is the general public, as consumers, whose interests are being allegedly undermined by advertising. GE's research determines that the "public" wishes to retain "freedom of information".

- the alliance, representing those businesses and organisations with a common interest in maintaining commercial freedoms, continues to be developed. Once the issue is generally known, the actual threat is well understood, and with every contact there is agreement to support the campaign.

- preparing a detailed set of argumentation and briefing papers to be used with targets, both at the academic and technical level, and also at the populist level.

- preparing an advocacy campaign to be carried in the quality press and business magazines, supported by PR, lobbying and media relations campaigns. It has been agreed that some media space is to be funded by the media owners themselves.

GE is reminded that an advertising industry advocacy campaign had been running, intermittently, over the last few months, and a decision is made to continue with this, but at a higher spend level in the interim. This will help to maintain the advertising industry's identity and arguments in the public's mind whilst a new campaign is developed.

Communications Plan

The communications plan optimises the impact of GE and associated industry arguments through an integrated political, media and PR programme, advocated by an alliance of interests. The plan is to be carried out through all appropriate media and PR channels, with a high spending level for the campaign.

The purpose of all this activity is to bring political pressure on the decision-makers, and by extending the case to the public GE believes that politicians will be obliged to listen to the arguments against an advertising ban.

The key elements of the communications plan are a direct media advocacy campaign, a lobbying programme, a media relations programme, a PR campaign – and of course, sufficient funds and commitment by all concerned. Note: all these key elements have been detailed in earlier Chapters, and are not repeated here.

The distinguishing feature of the whole campaign is the alliance of interests, crossing borders and markets and integrating different types of businesses, but because of this the co-ordination of the plan turns out to be more complex than usual.

Conclusion

The power and arguments of the alliance are sufficient to carry the day, and the threat of an advertising ban moves back to beyond the horizon.

The Future

The lesson has been learned this time! Business as a whole has become aware of the potential threat to its commercial freedoms that can be proposed by activists working closely with elements of government, and few of those concerned are left under any misapprehension as to the issue becoming live again.

Greater resources are allocated to early-warning systems, and the tracking of the issues. A specific agreement is reached between the alliance members to continue with a more effective information/intelligence network, and with a background campaign stressing the positive aspects of advertising.

REMINDERS!

- **SPECIMEN PA CAMPAIGN**

- **ISSUE DEFINED**

- **OBJECTIVE SET**

- **STRATEGY AGREED**

- **PREPARATORY WORK**
  - Legislative powers identified
  - Common ground identified
  - Contacts updated
  - Argumentation updated
  - Agencies briefed
  - Attitudes researched
  - Dedicated campaign team

- **OUTLINE PLAN**
  - Targets Defined
  - Detailed argumentation
  - Alliance developed
  - Advocacy campaign
  - PR campaign
  - Lobbying campaign
  - Media relations campaign

- **COMMUNICATIONS PLAN**
    - Integrated political, media and PR programme
    - High level spend
    - Complexity / organisation

- **FUTURE**
    - Issue will reappear
    - Information resources strengthened
    - Background campaign

Integration, Co-operation and Co-ordination

chapter 5

Integration, Co-operation and Co-ordination

By this stage, the key steps to take in developing a public affairs campaign have been marked out, and I have outlined the planning and development of a specimen campaign. In all of this, I have tried to emphasise the importance of – DO IT NOW! – in order to demonstrate that only rarely do you have the luxury of taking it all logically step-by-step, and that because of this almost everything that needs to be done has to be done *now*.

But, there is another important point to make before we go further, and that is to ensure you give proper thought to the integration, co-operation and co-ordination of all your campaign elements.

The implementation of the ideas suggested in this report calls for a high degree of liaison and co-operation within the relevant functions in your business, between associated businesses and any alliances and/or trade associations, and a high degree of integration between the various elements of your campaign. This integration needs to be structured in at an early planning stage to ensure that, firstly, all businesses and functions concerned are familiar with and committed to the objectives and strategy of the campaign, and the means by which they will be achieved.

Second, to ensure that all involved are fully supportive at all times, and have the facilities and resources available to carry out the tasks agreed with them – which is not always the case in practice. Also, businesses and functions in neighbouring markets need to be kept informed of issues and actions in the event that regional action becomes necessary. But be aware that it is quite possible that the size of other markets and the expertise and resources available in them will differ significantly from those with which you are directly concerned.

In developing a structured plan for integration, the guide-lines below will help:

- at the beginning of the planning stage establish a realistic timetable, and do not be too optimistic. Despite the inevitable pressure to hasten matters along, both from within and without, do not give way so much that your objectives are compromised, and the campaign put at risk.

- in developing the various campaign elements, use a co-ordinated approach. The different elements should support each other in timing, message and content so that a synergistic effect is achieved.

- look closely at your campaign themes. Be sure that they complement and integrate with each other, particularly if you are running a multi-media campaign. Do not fall into the trap of allowing different agencies and consultants on your team to promote themes which are markedly different, and which do not complement each other.

- control your resources – you are the leader. Apart from the necessary control of campaign themes, consider the alliances and third-parties you may be working with – try to ensure that their themes are at least complementary with your own. For good reason, they will not be the same in many instances, as this may compromise their credibility and authority.

- designate an executive(s) to be responsible solely for co-ordination and integration, including the exchange and distribution of documentation. This person should continuously monitor development of the action plan for the campaign, should notify all concerned of the development stages, and draw attention to improvements that could be made. The need to liaise with associated businesses and colleagues in other markets would also fall into this area, and may be of particular assistance to them in developing their own campaigns, and building an alliance of interests.

- note that "winning campaigns" integrate all elements of the campaign. Analysis of campaigns that stand out will generally identify that "integration" between and with all elements was of immense importance in the achievement of the objectives. Be sure to give enough time to "integration".

REMINDERS!

- **INTEGRATION OF CAMPAIGN ELEMENTS**

- **KEY FACTORS:**
    - Establish realistic timetable
    - Use co-ordinated approach
    - Consistent campaign themes
    - Control resources
    - Executive(s) for Integration
    - "Winning campaigns" integrate all elements

Building Confidence

Building Confidence

One of the prime difficulties in campaign planning is sometimes to convince your own management to support your campaign, or even to get them to the stage of recognising the strength of the issue or threat facing them. There may be industry or in-house arguments against public affairs campaigning, ranging from not being able to raid the marketing budget, to not raising our heads above the parapet, the Chairman is lunching with the Minister, all the way to masterly inactivity.

Of course, sometimes these are the right courses, but too often they are the resort of complacent or unaware management. There may be a proper time for masterly inactivity, but if so then it will be because it represents a considered decision, with all the arguments taken into account, and not one taken by default.

But once a decision is made to "GO", then is the time to go full speed with all the arguments deployed, with all available media, with all the authority that can be brought to bear, and with appropriate expenditure and duration. All this taken together will help to build confidence in your team and in the business. Negatives will be minimised with such a course of action.

Your business may be new to running public affairs campaigns, and a lack of confidence is the last thing you need. With a full-blooded campaign agreed, though, you should consider two factors in particular to build confidence:

- the need to build confidence with your business colleagues by communicating the perceived problem and your plans to them, and arranging for them to have the opportunity to make contributions. In practice, it is probable that many of them will have been involved in assessing the risks and impact of the issue, and in contributing to the campaign.

Other important audiences in this context are general management, employees, your trade association(s), and of course, the in-house and out-house campaign team (this has been covered earlier). You should also consider advising selected media in this same context; they will find out once employees and others are informed, and it is far better that they are briefed by you than find out covertly. Remember that you know more than they do, so you can observe proper confidentiality.

- your own management and leadership will be under scrutiny, and you can help this aspect by being seen to:

    - set clear objectives

    - being realistic in your planning and timing

    - measuring your attainments

    - motivating your team and colleagues

Planning and running a public affairs campaign will give you and your team a great deal of visibility in your business, and possibly in the industry. The proper management and leadership of your team and of the campaign will stand you in good stead when the attainments come to be assessed. One way of recognising that the campaign has been successful is to observe that all sorts of people will come out of the woodwork and try to jump on the bandwagon. If it is not seen as successful then you can rely on some previously valued colleagues jumping your ship, and having the bullets fired at you from both sides.

REMINDERS!

- **BUILDING CONFIDENCE**

- **MINIMISING NEGATIVES**
  - All arguments deployed
  - Use all appropriate media
  - Authoritative tone
  - Appropriate expenditure

- **WORKING WITH COLLEAGUES**
  - High profile
  - Management
  - Leadership

Some Conclusions

chapter 7

Some Conclusions

The world is changing and business has to change with it to optimise the opportunities available. On the one hand the business world is being stimulated by a number of global factors such as financial deregulation, emerging markets, low inflation, and new technologies, yet on the other hand business is being restrained by such factors as political conflict, deficient infrastructures, and trade imbalances. Acting as an undercurrent to all this is the rise of regional government, as sovereign states become increasingly demoted in stature.

While the increasingly regional, if not global, nature of many of today's markets is undoubtedly opening up new opportunities, business faces many more legislative and regulatory barriers and restrictions than before. It is against this background that business decisions must be made, and amongst these are those concerned with planning and running public affairs campaigns - the subject of this report.

We must all learn to live, to adapt and change, and to thrive in this environment. Your ability to recognise and adapt to this global business warming will determine the level of confidence inherent in your campaign - and its degree of success. Remember - if you bring all the skills you can to your public affairs campaign then the luckier you will be!

- **CONCLUSIONS**
  - **Change – and thrive**
  - **Global business warming**

On a practical note, here are a few pertinent reminders on which to end and which sum up the advice in this report:

REMINDERS!

- **DO IT NOW!**

- **DO's:**
    - Plan ahead
    - Get allies on your side early
    - Keep your team well briefed
    - Maximise media opportunities
    - Be realistic in timing, achievements and expenditure
    - Pace the campaign

- **DONT's:**
    - Leave it all too late
    - Concentrate on one medium only
    - Spend too little / expect too much

- **REMEMBER!**

THE MORE YOU DO THE LUCKIER YOU WILL BE!

Appendix I
The UK Legislative Route: Parliamentary Proceedings for Passage of a Typical Bill

Appendix II
Notes on the European Union Legislative Process

Appendix III
Further Reading / Useful References

appendices

The UK Legislative Route: Parliamentary Proceedings for Passage of a Typical Bill

appendix I

The UK Legislative route: Parliamentary Proceedings for Passage of a Typical Bill

November

Bill announced in the Queen's speech.

December

First Reading in the Lords – a purely formal announcement. The Bill is published.

December

Lords Second Reading – a debate on principles.

January/February

Lords Committee Stage - when the whole House sits as a Committee and debates the Bill in detail.

March

Lords Report Stage - amendments are still possible.

Lords Third Reading

April

First Reading in the Commons

May

Second Reading in the Commons – with full debate on the principles.

Committee Stage - with line by line examination of the Bill. Amendments moved.

June

Report Stage – further amendments may be moved, or changes made in Committee can be reversed by a vote of the whole House.

Third Reading – Short debate.

July

Lords consideration of Commons amendments, and Commons reconsideration of Bill if Lords re-amend it.

Royal Assent.

Late July/mid-October

Summer recess.

October

If the Bill did not receive the Royal Assent in July, then the final stages are taken now.

Notes on the European Union Legislative Process

appendix II

Notes on the European Union Legislative Process

The passage of legislation in the Community involves a complex and often lengthy process of consultation and agreement. In brief, the Commission makes proposals, the European Parliament gives opinions and proposes amendments, and the Council decides.

All of these institutions provide opportunities for business to become involved, and specifically for lobbying purposes.

Only the Commission can propose legislation, although the Council may request the Commission to undertake studies and submit appropriate proposals.

A particularly important stage is when the Commission, in preparing its proposals, consults with "experts" and relevant business organisations. This is a vital stage for a business to advance its arguments.

Business is best advised by its own consultants, and in the UK the DTI provide helpful material eg "Influencing decisions in the European Community".

Further Reading / Useful References

appendix III

Further Reading / Useful References:

1. **Public Relations Techniques**
   Frank Jefkins – Butterworth Heinemann Ltd

2. **Campaigning**
   Des Wilson and Leighton Andrews – Hawksmere plc

3. **Successful Public Relations**
   Jim Dunn – Hawksmere plc

4. **The Regulatory Challenge**
   Bishop, Kay and Mayer – Oxford University Press

5. **Benn's Media Directory**

6. **Willing's Press Guide**

7. **European Marketing Pocket Book**

8. **Media Pocket Book**

9. **The Writer's Handbook**
   Macmillan Press Ltd

10. **Vacher's European Companion (quarterly)**
    Vacher's Publications Ltd

11. **Vacher's Biographical Guide**

12. Department of Trade and Industry (DTI) Information Service

Including on-line database of EU legislation, and "Influencing decisions in the European Community". UK Office of the European Commission

13. Commission of the European Union

Publications on the Legislative Process